ROBERT BOSMAN

4000 WEEKS

a life-changing novel

'The greatest danger for most of us
is not that our aim is too high and we miss it,
but that it is too low and we reach it...'

Michelangelo

Publisher: 2BeWise, Canada - The Netherlands

First edition: April 2011

ISBN: 978-0-9869328-0-9

Design: Robert Bosman

Editing: Will Menary

Editing services: Anders Schepelern (Wordy.com)

Typesetting services: BookGenie, India

'Like all other arts

the Art of Living

can't be mastered

without a deep understanding of its 'hidden laws'

without inspiration and imagination,

nor without continuous exercise.'

'Moreover, the Art of Living

can't be mastered

without a smile…'

'Everything should be as simple as it is,

but not simpler.'

Albert Einstein

This book is dedicated to YOU.

May it help you to live a great life...

You can!

Contents

<u>Note from the author:</u>

You will find '...' signs (the ellipsis) a lot in this book. Ellipsis have different meanings in different countries. I use them just to *indicate a pause*, a moment to contemplate for a few seconds about the previous text before moving on.

In some countries, '...' indicates that some original text of a quote was left out; but when I leave out original text, I will use '(...)' and when I *add* text to a quote, I will enclose those words between squared brackets: [*this text is added to the original quote*].

'While the spark remains
You must try and try again.
Don't give up, just change direction.
Turn around and start again…'

The Cats

THE TURNING POINT

It was the day that changed my life. But of course I had no clue about that when it happened.

I sat that day on a bench in Stanley Park, Vancouver. And I had never felt so sad... so very sad... My life had become a bad dream. Almost a horror movie... I still couldn't believe that the angry young man I was only two decades ago, had become quite suddenly such a misery... in poor health... substantially overweight... income too low, debt too high... and living in a frustrated relationship, holding down two boring, low income jobs that took all of my energy and most of my time. And always tired... so tired! I actually did not want to live any longer. More and more I found myself thinking about committing suicide, but I simply lacked the courage... or did I still have some hope for a better future? Even a reasonable future would take a miracle!

I saw the man from the very moment he came around the corner, on the path that ran around Stanley Park. Something about him touched me... I had no clue what it was, but I kept looking at him. Until, suddenly, he seemed to look directly at me. Embarrassed, I turned my head away, yet in my mind's eye I could still see him walking. Somehow I knew he was walking on a path that would bring him to me. On the one hand I didn't want to meet him: in the mood I was in, at that moment I didn't want to meet anyone! On the other hand something deep inside me thirsted to speak with that man... No, I actually just wanted to listen to him... Next moment I heard a pleasant voice say, *'Do you mind if I share this bench with you for a couple of minutes?'*

I looked up and there he was. Just an ordinary man at first sight... Somewhere in his fifties I estimated, and well dressed... He looked healthy, even strong. He had an open face with eyes sparkling like tinsel and a friendly smile. Nothing seemed to be extraordinary but his radiance. No doubt he was one of those few people with such a strong radiance that everyone seems to notice. I looked around me for a split second and saw several people watching us... no, watching him!

'Just feel free,' I replied to his question and without a word he sat down at the other end of the bench. He wordlessly watched the horizon for several minutes. I tried to ignore him but to be honest I liked sitting near him. It was actually a kind of a strange experience... as if my mind took on a piece of his quietness.

'What a beautiful day again.' he suddenly said after quite some time.

'Mmm,' I replied, not that enthusiastic.

The man looked at me for about half a minute but didn't say a word. Neither did I. I didn't look back, just focused on the horizon. I really hoped that he would say something... but my body language did not invite him to say anything. At least, that's what I thought...

He turned his head back to look at the horizon, like me, and was silent for a while. Then he said, 'At the risk of intruding, may I say that you don't look to be all that happy?'

Suddenly I was filled with emotions... strong, controversial emotions... I was pissed off that this perfect stranger had the nerve to involve himself with my private life! And at the same time I could almost cry from happiness that someone—finally—had taken notice of me and my state of life. Confusing! How to react? I was way too unsure and also too emotional to enter into a real conversation; but on the other hand I definitely didn't want to upset him.

He seemed to be able to read my mind. 'You don't have to say anything. I know where you are at... I have been there myself...,' and after a few more seconds he added: 'Congratulations!'

As if I'd been bitten by a snake I looked at him and almost shouted: 'Congratulations? Congratulations?? What do you mean for god's sake?' People within earshot looked towards us in surprise, but we both ignored them.

'Well...,' he said, 'it seems to me that you are at one of the darkest moments of your life... if not the darkest. That means that it's quite likely that things get better from now on. That was what I meant by congratulating you...'

I was astonished and looked at him in disbelief. And again he seemed to know, since he continued: 'I understand my words might sound weird and maybe even cheap, but I don't think they are. Only the future will tell us if I was right in saying what I just said. And I truly hope I was right. I apologize for having upset you and wish you a good day and a happy future.' He stood up to walk away but to my own great surprise I took his arm and said, almost in tears, 'Please don't go... Please don't go... Maybe you can help me to find my way to a better future and make your words come true...'

He looked deep into my eyes and said 'Young man, unfortunately I can't help you.'

It was as if all my life energy had been drained. Time stood still... Life seemed to have come to an end and I felt even more desperate than ever before... Then he added, 'But I know the man who can definitely help you.' And my heart was instantly full of hope again!

'Can you please introduce me to that man?,' I asked.

'Of course,' he replied, 'Even instantly, since at the moment he's right here and has been sitting next to me on this bench...'

I was confused for only a split second. 'You mean me?? That is a cheap joke you're telling me!' I almost shouted.

'No, young man, it's not,' he replied, 'On the contrary: it is the only real answer and the only real solution for all your problems. Please allow me to explain why...'

Once I'd cooled down and nodded, he sat down again and said, 'When you were born you got everything you would and will ever need to live a great life... But somewhere on your road through life you lost that treasure... Most people don't realize that their brains are shaped by their environment, literally, and every split second..., even right at this very moment. Most people don't know, either, that their brains can even turn off and on certain parts of their DNA! Your brains are extremely powerful and are your best companions in life; that is to say, if you use them well!'

'You should realize,' he went on, 'that your brains were literally shaped by your parents, your brothers and sisters, your school, your religion, your friends, your spouse, your boss and colleagues, your neighborhood, your language and culture, and so on and so on... Our brains keep our experiences as re-usable memories. All important impressions that we get from outside are kept in what are called our brains' 'neural networks,' the series of tiny 'threads' between our brain cells that are known as 'neurons.' Our just three pounds, or less than one and a half kilograms, of brains contain roughly a billion (1,000,000,000) neurons that are connected by about 100,000 kilometers of neural connections! Amazing, isn't it? But even more amazing is that most of those neural networks are created as a direct result of the influence of your environment and the people around you.'

He continued almost without a break and in a very convincing tone of voice. 'All these influences make some people happy, healthy and wealthy, but most people not. Being unhappy, unhealthy and unwealthy, like you obviously are, is just life's way to communicate the message that under the influence of so many often good willing people, you have lost your most important treasure: your real self. Your brain has literally become a strange mixture of their brains, and life is telling you that this 'borrowed brain' doesn't fit you. At first life's warnings were quite soft and polite. But the longer you neglected life's messages, the stronger its warnings became. It's obvious that you've got very strong warnings now: life urges you to re-wire your brain, to re-discover the real you and to re-design your life.'

He paused for a minute, observing my face, then nodded as if he was happy with what he saw and went on: 'Re-wiring your brain; re-discovering the real you; and re-designing your life... Those are not easy tasks, nor quick fixes. But you know...' and the Man's eyes got even more sparkling (yes, I write 'Man' from now on with a capital, both as a token of my respect for him and also since I still don't know his name!) as he went on, 'From the very moment you accept life's message and make a definite decision to become who you really are,— whatever it will take—from that moment on, your life becomes an adventure again and will reward you with new energy and inspiration, some of it even instantly!'

He observed me for several seconds and asked 'Do you recognize the wisdom and truth of what I just told you?'

I tried to say 'yes' but could only answer with a nod.

'OK, then you'd better start now. Don't waste the moment of recognized insight! I have a present for you. This might be all you'll need to succeed, plus your time and dedication of course...' From the pocket of his coat he took a small notebook and a nice wooden pencil with an eraser on top of it, and gave them to me.

'Good luck!' he said, 'My intuition tells me that you will find Your Way...' He shook my hand and walked away.

'Hey!' I said, 'Where can I find you if I need you?'

Without turning his head he replied 'Don't worry... If you really need me, you'll find me. But first you need to find yourself.'

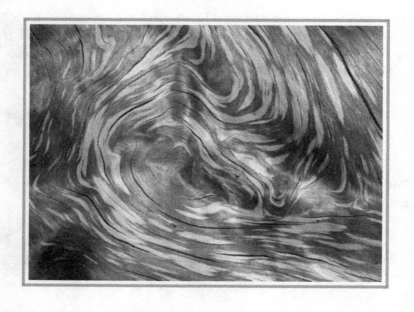

'To Be Wise or not to Be Wise…
That's the question.'

inspired by William Shakespeare

The Notebook

Deep in thought I walked home. A movie in my head replayed the meeting over and over, from the split second I first saw the Man walking around the corner until the last glimpse I saw of him as he walked away. Actually I was amazed by how sharp my memory was! I'd had severe concentration problems for over a year and normally my memory was, to say the least, not that good at all... But this was without doubt totally different...

As soon as I got home, I laid the notebook and the pencil on my desk, opened my computer and started typing everything I remembered of that amazing 20 or 30 minutes... In the previous chapter of this book you just read exactly what I wrote...

I printed a copy, took it to my bedroom and, lying on my bed, read it several times. Then I highlighted the keywords. It made me smile: I'd highlighted at least 80% of all words... Obviously the Man had not used more words than strictly needed!

I walked to the balcony and looked over the city. After a while I realized that the view I'd always found so boring, was not too bad at all... It was actually quite nice: I saw plants, trees, a part of the mountains and a little bit of the ocean... I saw children playing and the weird dance of all those cars... The colors of the clouds playing in the sky were just beautiful... I even liked the reflection of the sky and the clouds on so many of Vancouver's famous glass-wall buildings 'Maybe life is not so bad after all,' I heard myself saying softly, to myself, and much to my own surprise. There was little doubt that the meeting had changed my mood... substantially!

But suddenly a whole series of worries and fears came back and overwhelmed my thoughts and feelings, as a big wave destroys a sand castle... I could feel the pain in my chest and stomach again, the same pain that kept me sleep-deprived for so many months... Had my experience from that day just been a castle in the air? Just the wishful thinking of a desperate old fool?

Confused I walked inside. I was taken aback to see that the notebook was opened! I was quite sure that I'd left it closed. Magic? Or had it just fallen open as books can do? But hey…! Wait a moment… The notebook was not entirely empty, as I had thought! In a strong, clear handwriting, that seemed to mirror the Man's self-confidence, I read at the top of the open page the words:

4000 weeks

The remainder of the page was empty.

I stood frozen for a while… Then I took up the notebook and let its pages run through my fingers. There were some words on every 5–7 pages; all pages were empty besides those few words. It was like a book with the chapter titles only… That couldn't be a coincidence… Was it an invitation to write down my own thoughts about the various subjects mentioned in the titles? In some way that wouldn't surprise me at all. I looked at my newly typed notes and re-read one of the last things the Man had said during our 'meeting at the bench': *'I have a present for you. This might be all you'll need to succeed, plus your time and dedication of course…'*

At the moment he'd said that and given me the notebook, I had the impression that it was just a regular, empty notebook. But with those titles or headings—as I called these few lines in the notebook—in it, it actually made much more sense that the notebook could be 'all I needed to succeed.'

I wondered why the titles appeared in two colors. Two titles were in red: *Scientific Inspiration* and *Personality Matters!* All others were in a deep dark blue, almost black. I took my computer again and typed out all titles in the notebook, using the same two colors.

I printed the overview and thought about it for a while. It seemed quite obvious to me, that the two red titles were two chapters and all black titles were just headings or subtitles within those chapters. Suddenly I 'knew' for sure that this notebook and its mysterious titles were the Man's way to challenge me to 'dive' into these titles… to research them… to contemplate each of them and the two chapters as a whole… and, of course, to write down my own notes in the notebook…

And that is exactly what I decided to do. And you know: instantly after this decision my mental energy went back to the level I experienced when I was standing on the balcony earlier looking at the city. A kind of 'energetic peace' came over me. And I liked it, a lot!

Then some other words came back. I looked at my notes, and there they were: '*From the very moment you accept life's message and make a definite decision to become who you really are,—whatever it will take—from that moment on, your life becomes an adventure again and will reward you with new energy and inspiration, some of it even instantly!*'

He couldn't have described my mood any better…

A bit later I realized that in my excitement about the notebook, I was neglecting the two other 'ingredients' the Man mentioned: *time* and *dedication*! I took my calendar and within a few minutes made some more decisions:

• The May Long Weekend was in less than three weeks. I decided to expand it to a full four days dedicated to my new challenge: finding the meaning of the titles in the notebook, and writing down in the notebook my discoveries.

• I decided to spend that weekend on Salt Spring Island, one of the Gulf Islands close to Vancouver. I hadn't been there since my youth, but still had great memories. A perfect setting for some life-changing work!

• I would use the days before the coming May weekend to prepare for the trip, to buy some books that could help to 'decipher' the notebook's titles and to do each day some initial research on the web.

• And last but not least: I would try to meet the Man one more time before going to Salt Spring Island.

-o-o-o-o-

The last decision led to disappointment. Several times I returned to 'our bench' in Stanley Park, stayed there quite a long time, but saw no trace of the Man at all. Although I was, to be honest, slightly disappointed, I realized that it might be too early for a next meeting. He had said that I would find him when I really needed him. And let's be honest, I would not really need him as long as I had not spent sufficient 'time and dedication' working on the notebook. So I postponed my desire for a meeting and concentrated on what I could do.

Every day I spent substantial time researching the various titles and subheadings in the notebook. Although my mood was still a roller-coaster, the daily work on my new mission kept me in a quite good mental and physical condition, at least compared to that of just a few weeks ago.

My first research activity was to go to search engines for all titles in the notebook. I used Google Bookmarks to make four lists of interesting websites and documents I found: one about 'Science and Miracles,' one about 'Personality Matters,' the third one with interesting books, courses, audio and video and the last one with other interesting websites which I came across.

It took me several days—actually evenings, since I had to work during the day—to create good lists, but the time was very well spent: I learned a great deal 'on the go' and found a lot of inspiring and encouraging resources.

As soon as the booklist was ready, I made up my mind which ones I would buy as physical books and which ones as ebooks. Chapters on Robson Street, by far my favorite bookstore in the city, had most books in stock, luckily enough.

Sooner than expected came the day of departure. I had booked a nice Bed and Breakfast on Salt Spring Island—amazing how many B&Bs there are over there!—and arranged that I could check in early and check out late; which really gave me nearly four whole days. In order not to destroy that advantage by long ferry trips, I allowed myself the luxury of flying to Salt Spring by sea plane. Salt Spring Air took me, in less than half an hour, from downtown Vancouver to lovely Salt Spring Island. When I asked the pilot's name, he answered with a smile, 'My name is St.Clair but most people call me just *Saint.*' I smiled as well, but for a double reason: to start my new mission by a flight with a 'saint' as the pilot was just a very nice coincidence. Or maybe even a token...

In the next two chapters you will find my notes on the various titles and subtitles in the notebook the Man gave me.

A tip: *It might be worthwhile to buy a small notebook yourself and make some notes while you are reading and every time when a thought 'pops up'. Be aware that your mind normally digests experiences and other mental input over night and might present you with tremendous insights quite soon after rising... Without making notes you will forget most of these insights and that's a pity. How important a book might be, the reactions of your own mind are way more important!*

'Knowledge is ripened experience from the past.

Wisdom is ripened insight for the future.'

Robert Bosman

Scientific Inspiration

Although googling the words 'Scientific Inspiration,' resulted in many millions of websites, the results were quite confusing and actually didn't touch me. Far more inspiring to me was the list of all the subtitles in this chapter of the notebook, so I decided to concentrate on these. The first one in the notebook was:

4000 Weeks

When I googled this title, the first response was:

$$4000 \ weeks = 76.6614594 \ years$$

I realized instantly what this title meant: 76 years is about human life expectancy in much of the developed world.

Then it hit me: was that true? *Was life only some 4000 weeks???* I had already spent about half of that...The number became even worse when I realized that I would sleep about a third of the remainder, which gave me only some 1300 weeks net to go. Only 1300 weeks! And oh boy, each week goes so fast!

Amazing that by just 'saying' the same fact in a different way (in 'weeks' instead of 'years' as we normally do), I got, instantly, a deeper understanding and much improved grasp of the true significance of this fact. *Rephrasing suddenly seemed an interesting mental tool.*

The good news was that a lot of books and websites show that *we can substantially increase the likelihood of living a lot longer than the average* by living more consciously, and by changing some habits; moreover these changes will improve our quality of life as well.

Searching further on this subject I found some information that was both shocking and hopeful at the same time: it was an article in the *Vancouver Sun* of February 5, 2011 with the title *'Many cancer deaths could be prevented, health experts say'* (google this title to read the full article). The article was triggered by simultaneous press releases of the World Health Association (WHO) and the World Cancer Research Fund (WCRF). The main conclusion was that about 30% of all cancers in countries as diverse as China, USA, Brazil and the UK could be prevented by 'simple life style changes'! That is in total about 1,000,000 preventable cancer deaths in these countries… every year! I made some calculations; my estimate, based on this article and some other official statistics, is that *globally more than 9,000,000 lives can be saved… yearly…* And that figure only includes deaths from cancer, heart diseases and diabetes!

Although these figures in themselves are shocking, they nevertheless might be very much underestimated: a web article called 'The Cancer Food Connection' on www.Alive.com—a website which is as good as its monthly Canadian magazine *Alive*—shows that the US Surgeon General stated as early as the 1980s that 70% of all North Americans are dying from diseases directly related to their eating habits. 70%! Since then, the incidence of diet-related illnesses and deaths has been steadily rising…

My main lesson from this was quite obvious:

• Rephrasing is a good method to open the mind;
• Life goes far faster than we normally realize;
• Yes, we normally can add years to our life, and life to our years;
• I should drastically change most parts of *my* life style.

I realized that the last lesson was easier to learn in theory, than to do in everyday life. And I was obviously not the only one who had come to that conclusion: the *Vancouver Sun* article quoted Ms Rachel Thompson, Deputy Head of Science of the WCRF, who said: *'It's all very well us saying 'This is what you need to eat and this is how much physical activity you need to do.' But we need to make it easier for people to make those changes. Everybody has a role in that: from international organizations, to governments, to people themselves.'*

That quote illustrates the essence of both the global health problem and my own one: I had KNOWN already for years that I should change major elements of my life and my life style, but so far it hadn't led to me DOING IT! I had no clue why… But I had become convinced I should find the answer and make it happen, SOON!

The next subtitle or subheading in the notebook was:

ARTS AND SCIENCE

My first impression of this subtitle was that Arts and Science were two quite different things. I was amazed by how wrong that impression was! Googling 'arts and science' I found that many, many universities have a *'College of Arts and Sciences.'* In those colleges Arts are not the *'fine arts,'* such as painting, sculpture, music, dance and theatre, but the *'liberal arts,'* or simply said: *'the art of clear thinking, sound reasoning, proper communication and applied wisdom.'* I was surprised to learn that the notice of 'liberal arts' in education goes back about twenty three centuries as it originated from the ideas of the old Roman and Greek philosophers. Liberal Arts were implemented about 1000 years ago in the first European universities and aimed to *develop the 'human being' first*, before allowing him to specialize in any profession. Grammar (proper language), rhetoric (the fine art of speaking), dialectics (the fine art of arguing and negotiating), mathematics, philosophy (literally: the love for wisdom), astronomy and music were all essential subjects of the Liberal Arts. Moreover, physical health and strength were core parts of education as well; daily sport was the rule!

Wow...! When we compare these ideas about education to what is done today in our schools and modern universities, our programs seems to lack some very essential elements.

Using the search engines further I found the book 'The Element' by Sir Ken Robinson, and also his website, and his at once comic and serious TED-lecture; Sir Ken pleads for a *'revolution in education'* that takes way more time for the development of the 'whole human being' instead of mainly educating the brain or, put more precisely: educating mainly the left (logical) side of the brain. *'The Element'* is a must read!

'But why,' I thought, 'was this *Arts and Science* subject mentioned in the notebook anyway?' Then I realized: the message was not to society, or for education, but in the first place directed to me! I should develop myself much more as a 'whole human being.' I should practise the Liberal Arts, since these Arts were a part of my own liberation... I was the one who should practice the art of thinking, speaking, arguing, acquiring wisdom, and so on! Since the topic was not limited to the Liberal Arts only, I decided to bring more Fine Arts into my life as well.

I was absolutely sure I had found the right meaning of this title in the notebook and went on to the next one:

YOUR MIRACULOUS 'RAW MATERIAL'

At first the idea behind this title was a hard one to understand. Googling both the whole title as well as all kinds of related words and word combinations gave so many different results, that it confused me. I stopped abruptly and went for a walk. A bit later I found myself walking through Stanley Park... Maybe my subconscious directed me that way, hoping to meet the Man and to raise some questions. But... no meeting. Obviously enjoying the walk, the weather and being outdoors in spring, I happily forgot about the 'raw material' puzzle.

But as soon as I came home and opened the door, I realized that this subtitle in the notebook needed to be seen in relation to the following subtitles of the same chapter: my miraculous DNA, Body, Brain and Soul. No doubt this title was pointing to something that even comes before DNA. That couldn't be anything else than 'our smallest parts': the molecules, elements, atoms and subatomic particles of which everything in the universe, you and me included, is composed.

Energized by this discovery and absolutely convinced of my sudden insight, I started my exploration into these subjects. Only later, while working on the next chapter, I learned that my decision to forget about the meaning of this subtitle for a while and instead to go for a walk, actually had given my *conscious mind* some time to relax by handing over the 'pending question' to my *sub-conscious mind*. My sub-consciousness started processing the pending question instantly and came up with the best answer when I came home. No, that is no hocus-pocus at all... It is just a part of how our mind operates; more about this in *Personality Matters*!

Our smallest parts

Of course I had learned something about atoms, molecules etcetera at school, but no doubt there were new insights, so I decided to re-start my research as if I knew nothing about the subject. I realized that

I should not only look at scientific facts, but should keep my mind's eye open for the 'miraculous' aspects as well.

Although there seemed to have been quite some discoveries about 'sub-sub-atomic' particles, the essence of what I had learned at school had not changed very much at all. Atoms are still considered to be the basic unit of all matter. Atoms consist of a central core (the 'nucleus'), composed of different sub-atomic particles (protons and neutrons) and surrounded by a cloud of electrons. Protons have a positive electrical charge, electrons a negative one, while neutrons, as the word indicates, have no charge at all. Electromagnetism binds the electrons to the core of the atom.

Atoms can be best visualized as a huge, dark, silent and empty space—scientists call it 'the quantum space'—in which a kind of uninterrupted 'fireworks' is happening, the 'dance' of mainly electrons around the core of the atom. Like real fireworks, the lightning particles are only 'visible' for a very short time and fill only about one ten thousandth of the space in our atoms; the remainder of this quantum space is more or less empty.

Atoms differ according to the number of protons, neutrons and electrons they have. Only 118 different atoms are known at the moment. Molecules are groups of atoms and may consist of just one kind of atom, in which case we call them 'elements,' like oxygen (chemical formula O_2), or are composed of different atoms like water (chemical formula H_2O).

Atoms can be understood as being at the border of matter and energy: sub-atomic parts can actually be understood better as being *energy*,' while molecules can be understood better as being *matter*.' Matter is actually 'organized energy.' It is the *information* embedded in the smallest particles—like the number of protons, neutrons and electrons in an atom and their electrical charge—which is used to organize the energy into ever changing matter... *The raw material of the universe is energy and information!*

Most non-living matter is composed of elements and relatively simple molecules; living cells and organisms are built of quite complex molecules.

It has to be said that, since my schooldays, particles have been defined with names like Hadrons and Quarks, that are even smaller than sub-atomic particles. But I assume that the above is sufficient to get a feeling for our Miraculous Raw Material.

So, at the deepest level everything is a thrilling field of space, energy and information: the universe, the earth, the mountains, the sea, our houses, our body, our cells... on the level of our 'raw material' it's all one big field of energy and information, jokingly sometimes called 'the quantum soup.' It's the energy that causes everything in the universe to keep moving. It's the information that causes this tremendous, continuous movement to stay tied together as 'a whole.'

Atoms and our senses...

When we look, for instance, to a mountain, our eyes actually don't see that mountain at all. Our eyes just register the continuous flow of light waves (or fotons) that reflects from that mountain and send these 'impressions' to our brain. *It's our brain that 'translates' these impressions into a format we can better understand: a mountain...* The same happens in all of our senses. Our senses register the *energy* and *information* of everything; it's the brain that translates these impressions into familiar images, sounds, tastes, smells and touch. We never experience anything on the atomic or molecular lever, although that is exactly what our senses do; we experience most things as physical objects or coming from physical objects. The *'formatted reality'* that our brain produces is so easy to understand, that we even call it *'reality'* and most of the time totally forget about the existence of the deeper level of which all reality is composed.

For most people it's hard to understand that what we assume to be *'objective reality'* is actually our *subjective interpretation* of sensory input. Moreover, it is per definition impossible that two people get exactly the same sensory input. Two people have seen the same accident, but the simple fact that they were standing a meter apart makes their sensory input different. Moreover, brains can only process a part of all the impressions they get and each brain differs in the way it selects which information (which details of the accident in the example) it registers and which not. Every policemen can tell you how different the stories are of witnesses to any accident. Therefore, the judge who asks you to tell 'the truth and nothing than the truth' actually asks you something that is impossible...

In other words, in our awareness reality is limited to what we experience, but actually 'reality' is always composed of two levels: the level we *can* experience and the level we *can't* experience. David Bohm called the part of reality our brain can experience *'the explicit order'* (the order folded out), while the *'the implicit order'* (the order folded in) can't be experienced by our brain directly. Since these words are still quite difficult, I have called them *'the visible reality'* and *'the invisible reality.'* *It's important to realize that it's the invisible reality that creates the visible reality and not the other way around!* If that sounds a little bit weird, just think about the atomic bomb and nuclear energy: the energy that is 'folded into' the atoms becomes a huge force as soon as it is 'folded out.'

If we don't realize these deeper aspects of reality, we become prisoners of our senses. Fascinating, isn't it?

A bit of Quantum Physics

As if these aspects of our 'raw material' are not yet miraculous enough, I found the ideas behind the so called 'quantum physics' quite fascinating as well. Quantum physics became important with a scientific article written by Albert Einstein in 1905 about the essence of light. At that time most scientists adhered to the assumption that light was composed of waves and matter was composed of electromagnetic particles (sub-atoms). In his article, Einstein—only 26 years old at that moment—explained that light can be waves at one moment and particles of light (called photons) at the other moment: light had two totally different 'characters.'

That was a shocking new vision: the so called physical reality was not confined to *one* explanation that was *true or not*, but had *two* different, mutually exclusive 'characters' that could *both* be true, but not at the same time. Moreover Einstein proved that the *likelihood* that light would behave as a particle or as a wave, could be *predicted* with the then very new *Quantum-theory* of Max Planck. Planck had argued that atomic energy does not change gradually, but with small, constant jumps. Just to get a better understanding, suppose that the temperature in a room does not rise gradually (from 21 to 22 and then 23 and 24 degrees, for example) but jumps from 21 to 24 degrees instantly, while 22 and 23 degrees just don't exist... That is exactly how atomic energy behaves: it jumps and these jumps cannot be predicted with certainty; only the *likelihood* of these jumps can be predicted. *In other words: on the atomic level there is no certainty, only likelihoods!*

It took more than 30 years before science could really prove that Einstein was right, but without doubt he was. Physics had changed forever and many 'puzzles' in physics could be solved using Einstein's explanation of Planck's Quantum Theory. It even became the foundation for nuclear energy and the atomic bomb. Many years later Einstein received a belated Nobel prize for his article. Not bad for a guy who only a few years before had been refused as a student at university and could hardly find a job...

Please don't think that I can really understand the above completely; only a few people in the world can. But undoubtedly I found substantial new scientific information that opened my inner eye to our 'miraculous raw material.'

So it was time to move on to the next chapter subheading:

YOUR MIRACULOUS DNA

Reality becomes even more miraculous when energy, information, atoms, elements and molecules form living cells. The change from 'just molecules' to living cells is a quantum jump in itself... It took me some time to get a basic understanding of DNA, but, no doubt, it was worth the effort! The world of DNA is of an amazing complexity, yet composed of amazing simple elements. Just as in our 'raw material...'

Here is what I took away from my research in this subject:

All known living organisms have the same, very detailed 'blueprints' called DNA. The DNA the instruction book of the body. Actually the word 'book' is quite useful here: a book is composed of only 26 characters (in the case of the English language) which can be combined into many words. Words can be linked into sentences, which in their turn form the chapters of the book.

The *alphabet* of DNA contains only four characters, normally represented by A, T, C and G, the initial letters of the names of four specific molecules.

All '*words*' in the DNA language have the same length: 3 characters per word. But the number of words in each sentence can differ; a whole '*sentence*' of 'DNA words' is called a *gene*. Most genes contain the full detailed instructions about how the body can make its main molecules: 20 different *amino acids* and about the 25.000 *proteins*.

Proteins are essential parts of virtually every process within cells, and, of course, all types of proteins exists: enzymes, for example, are proteins used in the digestion of food; insulin is a protein used to maintain our energy level; other proteins are used in building muscles and skeleton, the creation of energy in our cells, and so on. *The role of genes is to give the orders or instructions while the role of each protein is to carry out a specific task.*

Very important to know, is that only 10 out of the 20 amino acids can be made by our body itself; the other 10 have to come from our food (and are therefore called the '*essential amino acids*'). So, *what* we eat is tremendously important, among other factors since *our food has to contain all 10 essential amino acids*. A lot of attention is given to *how much* we eat and 'calorie counting'; of course this is important as well, but new insights teach that what we eat and what foods we can better combine, is much more important. More and more evidence is coming out, revealing that people with a good balanced diet, a healthy mind and sufficient exercise, can more or less eat as much as they want—and still maintain a healthy weight.

The Human DNA is 'a book' with 46 chapters called *chromosomes*: 23 inherited from the mother and 23 from the father. Each chromosome contains a specific string of our total DNA. All chromosomes together contain about 25,000 genes, which in total are written with more than 6 billion 'characters,' which means that the average 'sentence' (the blueprint for one gene) contains roughly 80,000 words, totaling about 240,000 characters. Pretty long sentences, aren't they? To get some idea of the amazing amount of information:

The DNA in each of our 70 trillion body cells contains
the equivalent of 16,000 printed books
containing roughly 250 pages each !

Isn't that miraculous??? Each DNA string is 100% identical in each cell of our body; moreover, it's a unique mix of exact copies of the genes of our ancestors; only a few changes in the genetic structure have happened in the millions of year since the human DNA was formed.

About 99.99% of the DNA in all human being exactly the same...

If you want to know more about DNA, some good reads are *River out of Eden* (1995, Richard Dawkins) and *The Web of Life* (1997, Dr Fritjof Capra).

To be honest I always felt a little bit ambivalent about DNA: some books and articles write about it as if DNA determines almost everything in our life. But if that's the case, free will would not exist, which I can't believe to be true. Some other explanations consider DNA to be hardly important at all: they preach that whatever DNA you inherited, you can reach whatever you want, as long as you really go for it; which I really can not believe either. What was true? Contemplating these opposite approaches, I suddenly realized that reality might consist of 'quantum jumps' here as well: DNA might determine the *likelihood* that some things happen in our life, but both our *own decisions* and *our environment* have substantial input into what actually happens.

This vision is strongly supported by modern research. A young branch of biological science is even called *'epigenetics'* (literally: 'beyond genetics'); it studies 'all non-genetic factors that cause the organism's genes to behave differently.'

Only recently, we've learned that stress, mood and emotions
can even turn some genes on or off!

A quote from the Scientific American book *Brave New Brain* (2010, Judith Horstman): '[*Scientists*] *also found that distressing events can turn off the expression of genes for brain cell growth protein and thereby trigger depression and (…) may also underlie the pathology of schizophrenia, suicide, depression and drug addiction.*'

Wow…!

To put the main conclusion from all the above in the form of a metaphor: the basic components and wiring of a TV set determines that it is a TV and not a radio, but can't predict what will be shown on the TV's screen; what is visible on screen at any given moment of that TV set's 'life,' depend also on the selected channel and on what is broadcast. Likewise *my DNA determines that I am human and also the talents and limitations I have, but NOT what I make from my life.*

What I make from my life is based (1) on the *DNA* that I inherited, (2) on my own *decisions*, and (3) on my *interaction* with the people, objects, environment and activities around me. Since these same *3 key-elements* shape the life of all other living species, life's *reality* can best be understood as '*a staggering synchronicity, a simultaneous interaction of events and reactions on events, that are significantly related but have no discernible causal connection*'; this definition is inspired by the definition of synchronicity in Google Dictionary.

Be aware: *synchronicity* is very different from *coincidence*! With coincidence we are more or less the victims of what happens. We almost never are! In real life you and I have had quite some impact on whatever happens in each of our lives: we have made previous decisions that brought us to where we are now, we had a huge impact on selecting the people, objects, environment and activities around us, and last but not least, we have or have not used our ability to activate or de-activate parts of our genes, even when we were not aware of it. Since we had, and have, substantial influence on all *3 key-elements* that shape our life, it is at least naive to see life as just a series of coincidences. For exactly the same reason it is quite naive to see life as fully predestined. Both attitudes are simply too easy; perhaps even (some may argue) quite cowardly as well.

Real life is partly pre-destined (we got our DNA for example), *partly free will* (we make choices continuously) *and partly coincidence* (we have to deal with the influence on our lives of everyone and everything around us). Such a synchronistic—or if you wish 'holistic'—view of life does not exclude belief in a God, nor in his or her importance, but does not diminish our own importance, or that of anyone else, or of anything in the universe.

The book *Brain Facts* (2008, The Society for Neuroscience) states *'for example, that identical twins (who have exactly the same DNA) have an increased risk compared with non-identical siblings of getting the same disease. However, if one twin gets the disease, the probability that the other will also be affected is only 30 to 60 percent. Environmental influences include many factors such as toxic substances, diet, and level of physical activity but also encompass stressful life events.'*

> *We are not the prisoners of our DNA,*
> *nor of our destiny...*

For me, the above also has one more spiritual dimension: the scientific fact that we share the same DNA system with all life on earth, and that 99.99% of the human DNA is exactly identical in all human beings, proves that *there is one origin, one source of creation, one God* (whatever you call him or her)... *for ALL people.* Religions may be a different in the way they worship God, but using any religion to divide believers and non-believers and to set people against each other, goes completely against the idea that there is one God for all people...

> *Religion's role is to unite, never to divide...*

Religions and priests who preach anything else ought not to gain entry to your mind, just as poison should not get into your body.

Contemplating our 'miraculous raw material' and our 'miraculous DNA,' I become more and more convinced that God can better be seen as the creator of 'the amazing, opportunity- generating infra-structure that we call life,' and at the same time I become more and more convinced that it is up to us to make the quantum jumps... *it's up to us to live a great life.*

Is anyone still hesitating about the miracle of life? I am not. And we are only half away... So let's move on to the next subtitle:

YOUR MIRACULOUS BODY

All of us started with only one cell. That cell contained our DNA, 'our book of life': 25,000 genes described in about 2 billion 'words' and 6 billion 'characters.'

Then, the *cell division* starts, first slowly, but at double speed with each division. A new born baby has about 3,000,000,000,000 (3 trillion) cells, which means that in pregnancy about 127,000 cells per second are created! Each cell contains, of course, the full string of DNA, which means that in pregnancy the equivalent of about 2,000,000,000 (2 billion) '250 page books' per seconds are produced, or 762,000,000,000,000 (762 trillion) 'characters' per second...

We cannot even imagine such a process. But it happens, every second, in each of approximately 103,000,000 (103 million) women who are pregnant at the very moment I write this sentence...

About another 67 trillion cells are added in youth, bringing the total number of cells in an adult human body to about 70 trillion, about 10,000 times as many cells as all people on earth! Biological adulthood is reached at about age 16, after puberty is complete (some use other definitions).

But the miracle is even bigger: the cells in our body are constantly renewed. A few examples:

- a new stomach 'coating' every 5 days
- new grease in all fat cells every 3 weeks
- a new skin every 5 weeks
- a new liver every 6 weeks
- a new skeleton every 3 months
- fresh blood every 100 days

It is estimated that at least 98% of all cells are renewed regularly; the main exceptions are the neurons, or simply put, our brain cells.

When I had found these amazing pieces of information, I did some calculations and made some assumptions to get an impression of what the above means. You know what? Our body produces about 3 million new cells... every second! Some 18 thousand trillion (18,000,000,000,000,000) DNA characters per second, the equivalent of about 50 billion (50,000,000,000) printed books of 250 pages each. Per second!!

Consequently about the same number of cells have to die each second as well... Otherwise a body would literally explode within a few days. Although we normally prefer not to think too much about life and death, on a cellular level we are dying and being reborn all the time...

Please note that the numbers above only describe the miraculous 'production' of cells and DNA, not the thousands of processes in each cell, nor what is accomplished every split second of our life by the collaboration of cells in our body's organs. This doesn't even mention the impressive processes among the atoms in our body either, nor the exchange of energy, information and matter with the outside world...

All this and much more is done without any conscious effort. A sparkling fountain of life is in all of us. The trillions and trillions of activities in our body normally happen almost perfectly; mistakes are most of the time taken care of as well. *All processes are coordinated by an invisible conductor, the primordial intelligence of life, that we might call whatever we want, as long as we don't forget to 'see' its presence, to see the miracle...*

'Who doesn't believe in miracles, is not a realist.' said David Ben-Gurion once. My new insights about our miraculous 'raw material,' 'miraculous mind' and 'miraculous body' made me understand how right he was!

Contemplating the above, I started to realize that we normally experience our body as an object, something that just is as it is, and does not change that much. How wrong we are! *We can better see our body as a river, a continuous flow...* Our streaming bodies can be renewed quite fast... and destroyed as well. Just as we saw in our DNA, the body is influenced tremendously by our environment, but most of all by our own decisions: we can make and break our body. The choice is ours.

All choice is made in our brain or mind:

Mental Health is the key to the Quality of Life…

Which brings us to the next chapter subheading of the notebook:

YOUR MIRACULOUS BRAIN

The previous chapters had without doubt opened my mind for the miraculous in everyday life. Learning more about our brain just made the miracle bigger. I had always thought that all humans were born with a more or a less clever brain, a higher or a lower IQ, with more or fewer talents. I could not have been more wrong: *we all start with a 'given' brain at birth, but the real formation of the brain only starts then.* It's the environment—our parents, brothers and sisters, friends, school, religions, colleagues, boss, government, society—that shapes our brain almost completely when we are young. Only later on, do our own decisions exert more influence on the contents of our brain.

But talking about 'my own decisions': who is the 'me' that takes those decisions? Is that not the 'me' whose brain is already shaped by the environment? No doubt! So even when you take more control over your own life, it is quite an art to really be yourself. *Becoming who you really are, isn't very easy at all!*

Before I go on, I should share with you that I struggled a bit with the definitions of key words. I wondered for a while why this topic in the notebook wasn't called 'your miraculous *mind*' instead of 'your miraculous *brain*.' Looking up the definitions of 'brain' and 'mind' in some dictionaries, I found that 'brain' was considerably more specific, than 'mind.' The best description to use would be 'nervous system' since that includes the brain, the spinal cord and the nerves, which operate as one integrated intelligence. But no doubt 'your miraculous *nervous system*' would sound much too medical for the 'discovery tour' that the notebook headings clearly were triggering. So I came to understand that 'brain' is the right word here; the word 'mind' will be used more in the next chapter, covering Personality.

So let's explore our miraculous brain… On the one hand science has made great progress in brain research over the last decades. On the other hand the brain is such a miracle that even the best scientific knowledge is still very limited. Quoting Dr R. Douglas Fields, neuroscientist, senior investigator at the US National Institute of Health and author of the book *The Other Brain*: '*We have great new technologies, but still very very rudimentary knowledge [of the brain]*'

When scientific giants like Dr Fields confess their limited knowledge, I feel encouraged to share what I understand of our miraculous brain, as far as is relevant for this book.

The brain's structure

Our brain is composed or three main parts:

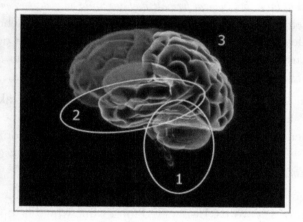

- *the lower brain* or primitive brain (see ellipse 1 in the picture), that includes the spinal cord and nerves. Most of all this part of our brain controls and supports the autonomous biological processes in our body, like heart rhythm, body temperature, blood pressure, digestion, hormone production, sex, reproduction and so on.
- *the middle brain* or limbic system (ellipse 2 in the picture). It is sometimes called '*the emotional brain*' and is responsible for most fundamental emotions, like joy, fear, anger, laughter, and so on.
- *the upper brain* or cerebellum, marked in the picture with a 3, is composed of two parts: *the left brain half* and *the right brain half* (formally called the two brain hemispheres) that are sharply separated but connected by an underlying bundle of nerve fibres called the

corpus callosum, and by Dr Jill Bolte Taylor called 'the highway for information transfer (2006, *My Stroke of Insight*). This upper part of the human brain differs the most from animal brains. Language, planning, reasoning, self-control, abstract thought, creativity, envisioning, pattern recognition and empathy are, among many others, all aspects of human capacities that mainly take place in the upper brain.

Brain cells and networks

As I said before, the brain — about 3 pounds in weight — contains roughly 100 billion (100,000,000,000) brain cells, called *neurons*.

Each neuron is connected to many others by two kinds of 'threads,' called dendrites and axons. The brain organizes information and creates meaning by literally making circuits of connections among brain cells. The total length of all these connections is indeed estimated at about 100,000 kilometres!

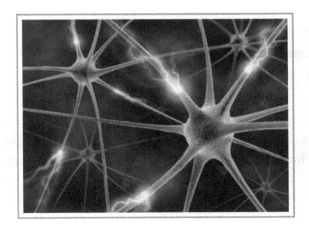

Most brain cells normally don't die. This enables us in theory to retrieve any information that has ever been stored in our brain. In *theory*, that is, since the retrieval of information always needs a 'trigger': we haven't thought in decades about our first year in school, for example, but as soon as we start chatting with one of our class mates from that time, it starts 'raining memories.'

The connections between neurons is not absolutely fixed: there is a tiny space between the connectors of two adjacent brain cells, called the *synapse*; when two brain cells connect an electrical charge 'jumps over,' or special chemicals, called neuro-transmitters are exchanged. This close but not fixed connection enables the same brain cells to be used in different connections.

How we create meaning

So far we have talked about the technicalities of the brain. But how does it create meaning? What actually is consciousness?

'Consciousness remains the largest mystery of all'

(quote from the Scientific American book *Brave New Brain.*)

Please read the following statements slowly, one by one, before looking at the next line or the related picture.

- 2
- 2%
- 2% increase
- 2% increase in sales
- 2% increase in sales this year
- 2% increase in sales this year, compared to minus 8 last year.

You may notice that these lines gradually become more meaningful; the first 3 lines have almost no useful meaning at all; meaning starts to evolve from the fourth line onward. In other words: meaning grows as we *relate* pieces of information. And that's exactly what happens in our brain: the neurons can be seen as the pieces of information that are related by the neural connections.

The same is visualized in the next picture: start with the number '2' and follow the arrows; you will read exactly the last of all the dotted sentences mentioned above. Each word in that sentence (and of course each word we know) can be understood as one neuron in our brain. By connecting the neurons a sentence can be formed, as you see in the picture. The neurons contain independent pieces of information, that only get meaning by the way they are connected to other pieces of information. So the brain organizes information and creates meaning by literally making groups (neural networks) of connections among brain cells.

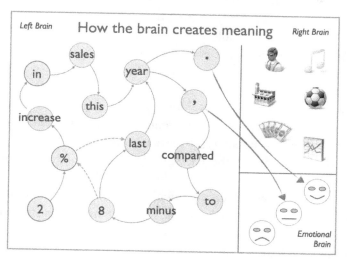

But there is more to see in this picture.

- Notice that some pieces of information are re-used, like the word 'year.' Re-using information in different neural circuits is an essential aspect of Brain Efficiency.

- Notice that the second part of the sentence that in used as an example does not mention the '%' sign; the sentence is *'compared to minus 8 last year'*. Nevertheless our brain normally interprets the incomplete wording as complete, by mentally adding the '%' sign after the 8; this is symbolized in the two dotted lines that start at the number '8' in the picture. This *auto-completion* is an important aspect of Brain Efficiency as well.

- All the words and their relations are at the left side of the vertical green line, symbolizing that our language center is normally located in *the left brain half* (or simply: *the Left Brain*). Characters, words and sentences in any language have to be processed one by one; our Left Brain could therefore in computer language be described as *a serial processor*: it can only store a very limited quantity (4-6) of sentences or thoughts at the same time.

- While we process information in the left brain half, *the right brain half* (or simply: *the Right Brain)* is heavily involved. The Right Brain can be seen as *a parallel processor* which processes a lot of information at once by seeing 'the whole picture.' It is also the Right Brain that continuously observes the body language and tone of voice of the speaker, seeking for inconsistencies in his message which might be of crucial importance for our survival. Moreover, the Right Brain completes all information by adding previous experiences, pictures, sounds, smells and tastes to each sentences the Left Brain processes. For example: the upper right corner of the picture above visualizes some activities of the Right Brain that adds some pictures to the sentence that starts with '2%': the Right Brain 'sees' an earlier picture of the speaker (the man with sunglasses), which came from a meeting at the speakers' company (the factory). The Right Brain sees as well that this company is the sponsor of the local soccer club (the ball) and knows that the word *sales* actually is used as an equivalent for money (the dollar bills). Moreover the Right Brain envisions instantly the graph of the development in sales while listening. And that's all at once!

- The *'Emotional brain'* plays a part in this process as well by connecting one or more emotions to the shared information, normally done at a pause in a sentence or at the end of it. *'2% increase in sales this year'* is in the example labeled as *emotion neutral* (see in the picture the connection between the *comma* and the neutral face symbol). That neutral emotion changes suddenly into a positive one after the second part of the sentence, since 2% increase in sales this year, is quite good compared to minus 8% last year; so the *dot* is connected with a smiling face.

Summarizing: *meaning* is 'the whole picture' created by *relating* pieces of *information* to each other by *thinking* (connecting more or less objective facts by the Left Brain) and by *feeling* (connecting personal experiences and values by the Right Brain and emotions and by the Emotional Brain).

Consciousness is being aware of the facts and their meaning. The same in a formula:

$$M = I \times R^2$$

Meaning = Information × Relation^{Thinking} × Relation^{Feeling}

The practical consequence:

Nothing *has* meaning.
We *give* meaning to everything, conscious or not.

We can *give* meaning, either by replicating the ideas that others planted in our brain, or by 'thinking for ourselves.' Of course it's best if we do the last, but in reality that is quite rare.

Brain flexibility

Brains are astonishingly flexible: a brain is able to regenerate itself and its functions and keep its stored information, even after very severe brain damage.

Karl Lashley trained rats to take a specific path through a maze; subsequently, he removed a part of the rat brains. What happened was astonishing: whatever part of the rat's brain was taken away, the rats remained able to find the way through the maze that they had learned before when they still had their full brain! Apparently the learned information was not stored in any specific part of the brain, but was available in any part of the brain...Experiments done by Karl Pribram proved that the same happens with the storage of visual information in the brain. Pribram's conclusion was that the brain works like a hologram.

A hologram is a kind of three-dimensional image like those seen in passports, bank cards and credit cards. If you look at a hologram from multiple angles, you see different images. Apparently many images are stored in the same place. It is difficult to understand that *each piece of a hologram contains all information of the entire object*: when a hologram, with for example, a lion's head on it, is broken into, say, four pieces, you still can see the whole lion's head in each of these four smaller holograms. Weird, isn't it?

If the brain stores information more or less in the same way as information is stored in a hologram, this could explain the results from the experiments done by both Lashley and Pribram. The biologist Paul Pietsch was initially a strong opponent of Pribram's holographic brain theory and developed a series of experiments to challenge Pribram's ideas. Pietsch swapped the hemispheres in the brains of salamanders, in the firm expectation that the salamanders would no longer be able to exercise their normal habits. The opposite happened: everything worked normally. Even when the brains were replaced upside down, functions stayed intact! A total of more than 700 similar experiments changed Pietsch from an opponent of the holographic brain theory into one of its biggest supporters.

The real importance of the above for us is not the holographic brain theory, but what we learn about the astonishing flexibility of our brain: it can overcome almost any problem! The work of Lashley, Pribram, Pietsch got an important real life validation in the touching story of Dr Jill Bolte Taylor: a high reputation neurologist herself, at age 37 she experienced a major stroke which destroyed most of her left brain half. But Dr Taylor not only survived and recovered, she used the unique opportunity for any professional brain researcher to document her experiences. In her book, lectures and website (just google her name and you will find them) she brings first hand a deeply touching insight into our miraculous brain. Never before had the huge differences between our left hemisphere and the right one been made so clear, or the tremendous cooperation between the seemingly very different parts of our brain. Her book *My Stroke of Insight* is an absolute 'must read' for anyone with brain problems and highly recommended for the rest of the world (^-^). Don't forget to look for her TED lecture!

Scientists wouldn't be scientists if they hadn't coined a new word for the tremendous flexibility and regenerative power of the brain: they call it *brain plasticity*. Summarizing in plain English:

> *Our brain is more than capable of helping us to re-create our life,*
> *even when we are in very bad shape. It's almost never too late!*

Learning and Emotions

The brain learns by creating new brain cells, but most of all by creating new connections (neuro-circuits) between existing brain cells. There are two triggers for learning:

- *The Emotional Shock*, which enables *instant learning*: the stronger the shock, the faster new neurons and neuro-circuits are created.
- *Repetition*, which enables *learning over time*: the neurons and neuro-circuits grow slowly, by each repetition, allowing for correction and gradual improvement in almost everything we put our attention to.

Learning by Emotional Shock serves often the main purpose of our brain: to help us—and the human species—to *survive*: things that shock us, normally need instant attention and the lesson needs to be kept, to avoid or prepare for future shocks.

Time for *a great practical tip* from the book *My Stroke of Insight* which I call *the Count-to-90-Rule*. Most of us have learned in our youth that when we become angry it's better to count to 10 before reacting. But better if we count to 90!…Why? Emotions differ substantially from feelings: *feelings* are mainly mental, while *emotions* are both mental and also expressed in our body: we cry, laugh, shake, freeze, frown and so on. It takes our body only a split second to express a strong emotion in trillions of relevant cells in our body; the technology of lie detectors, for example, is based on this amazing mind-body connection. But even more important to know is that it only takes 90 seconds for the body to flush away these emotions in the body: no trace of the emotion is measurable in the body after just 90 seconds!

This makes sense for our survival of course, since once the body is cleaned up, it is ready for a next emotion if needed. What stays on is the mental imprint of the emotion: while the body has forgotten the emotion after 90 seconds, the mind definitely has not. So, it will be hard, if not impossible, to get rid of any emotion in the first 90 seconds, but after that we have the option to let it go or to stay in the emotion, by re-using the track it made in our brain. In other words: *after 90 seconds, staying in an emotion, or not, is just a matter of choice. So, yes we can learn to manage our emotions!*

One more important fact about emotions is this. There is always a *trigger* for an emotion. That trigger can come from outside, as well as from inside our brain: suddenly remembering that we have forgotten a very important appointment, for example, can trigger a strong emotion. All mental input, whether from the inside or from the outside, passes two small brain parts in the middle brain, called the *amygdala* and the *thalamus*; they decide how important each incoming signal is and what to do with it. The incoming signal can be sent to the upper brain for 'normal processing' or can be sent (back) to the body instantly for direct action; in both cases these tiny little organs can add additional information and instructions to the signal and thereby 'order' specific reactions by the brain and by the body. The amygdala and the thalamus can be seen as the traffic agents of the nervous system, together taking care of the traffic on the mind-body highway.

'Why would I want to know that?' I hear you asking. Well, these two traffic agents are very very capable at doing their job in most circumstances. But when stress becomes too strong or lasts too long, they become—just like real-life traffic agents—overly tired and start making mistakes. The results can be devastating: whenever, for instance, we read about a father or mother that, to the utter dismay and shock of everyone who knows them, kills their whole family and often themselves, you can be pretty sure that their mental traffic agents were exhausted and made a final mistake, which is the case in most suicides, school shootings, terrorist attacks and so on... Does that mean that most of these awful things could be avoided? Yes! No doubt at all!

It 'only' needs *a healthy mind in a healthy body*, which has been the health idea for centuries, as coined by the ancient Roman philosophers: *mens sana in corpore sano*; both of these phrases in italics mean the same. All my research so far made me more and more aware that *mental health is the key* to health and to all other aspects of life: a healthy body, healthy relationships, a healthy job, a healthy bank account, a healthy society, a healthy economy, a healthy Planet Earth and so on. Would this be what C.G. Jung meant? He said:

> *'The world hangs on a thin thread: the psyche of men...'*

I think this world is as true for the 'big world' as it is for our personal world...

Learning by repetition

I realize I've written quite a lot about emotions and 'learning by emotional shock.' Let me only add a few things about 'learning by repetition.' This type of learning allows us in theory to learn everything we put our attention to. In theory... since there are some restrictions:

- The stronger the emotional stimulant, the easier the learning. It is hard to learn anything when we 'have to learn' because others want us to do so. Our neuro-circuits become stronger with right stimulus. Without the right stimulus we need many more repetitions to learn. With the wrong stimulus—being demotivated—learning by repetition is almost impossible; passing examinations becomes a hell since no doubt performance anxiety will hinder students tremendously. We see here one of the major problems at schools all over the world: they force students to learn without motivating them... No wonder that so many children don't finish school! They just cannot flourish in this system, but the system doesn't realize its own problem... Albert Einstein was so right when he said:

'It is a miracle that curiosity survives formal education'

- We can not only be forced to learn by outside factors, and fail, but by our own mind as well: if we want to master anything, while deep in our heart we don't believe we can, we start to fool and force ourselves, with exactly the same result as described in the previous paragraph.

Without a broad smile, we can't accomplish anything!

- Thirdly, even if we are highly motivated to learn, and believe we can but are not fully focused, we will learn only not as well. A person isn't likely to become a good plumber while making carpets most of the time...

Result = Intention realized by consistent attention

- Repetition can also be used to stay focused: writing down our intentions and plans and re-reading them regularly, is a profound tool for mental health and strength. Science calls this 'auto-suggestion,' a technology often mis-used in so called 'success literature.' Another Einstein quote:

Keeping the dream alive needs inspiration and transpiration

- Feedback is essential. Only by carefully comparing our aims with our results, in any aspect of life, can we get a solid impression about what we should learn and where we should improve.

Don't give up! Just change direction…

- Last but not least: repetition can be misused as well, not only by ourselves, but especially by others who want to manipulate or even brainwash us. And that is actually quite easy: just make sure people are in touch with a continuous stream of repetition. Repetition is the heart of successful advertising. Ceremonies, rituals, singing and dancing have been used for centuries in tribes, religions, governments, companies or any other kind of organization to keep people 'under influence.' Deepak Chopra, a true master of words, called these forces, expressed beautifully, *'socially programmed hypnosis.'* Pavlov coined a term for the same phenomenon. He called it 'conditioning.' Deepak Chopra, in one of his lectures I once attended, gave a striking illustration of how strong and dangerous the effects of conditioning can be: two groups of rats were given regular injections, one group with a substance that strengthens the nervous system, the second group with a chemical that breaks down the nervous system. During each injection both groups could smell camphor. After a while the injections were stopped, allowing both groups to return to their normal health level. Once all rats were healthy again, both groups got the smell of camphor at regular intervals, but didn't get any injections at all. And guess what? The first group gained strength just from smelling camphor! The nervous system of the second group, however, started to degenerate again, and some of them even died! Smelling the same substance triggered increased health to one group, death to the other; the only difference was in the mind! Shocking, isn't it? Well, be prepared for one more shock: exactly the same mind programming technology can not only be used by organizations, but by just about anyone to master your mind.

Think. Don't be thought!

Is the brain a kind of computer?

Definitely not! The brain is way more complex and sophisticated that any computer we know today. Although... the Scientific American book *Brave New Brain* comes with a very interesting approach: *the brain is not a kind of computer, but a kind of internet.* Which makes sense if we compare the brain cells with internet servers that contain information, and the internet network with the neural network. Interesting at least.

In the next chapter we will learn that it makes sense to compare the 7 most important functions of the brain with that of a computer, just to help understand those functions. But that doesn't mean that the brain is a kind of computer. The following quote from *Brain Facts* (2008, The Society for Neuroscience), not only confirms this point of view, it is a great finishing touch for this part of my notes: *'The human brain — a spongy, three-pound mass of fatty tissue — has been compared to a telephone switchboard and a supercomputer. But the brain is much more complicated than either of these devices, a fact scientists confirm almost daily, with each new discovery. The extent of the brain's capabilities is unknown, but it is the most complex living structure known in the universe. This single organ controls body activities, ranging from heart rate and sexual function to emotion, learning, and memory. The brain is even thought to influence the immune system's response to disease and to determine, in part, how well people respond to medical treatments.'*

'Ultimately, [the brain] shapes our thoughts, hopes, dreams, and imaginations. In short, the brain is what makes us human.'

The last sentence might give a little bit too much honour to the brain; shouldn't this honour be shared with our body and soul?

Your miraculous Soul

The Canadian neurosurgeon Dr Wilder Penfield conducted experiments with patients who had approved their cooperation in advance. The patient was brought under local anesthesia after Dr Penfield had opened up the patient's skull, allowing Dr Penfield to touch parts of the brain with a small instrument. Since the brain has no nerve cells as such, touching it causes no pain at all.

In one of his experiments Dr Penfield touched the patient's motor cortex, the part of the brain that controls body movement. The patient's left arm came up, whenever the Motor Cortex was stimulated in a certain place. Dr Penfield asked his patient what in his opinion had happened. The patient answered that his left arm came up without himself doing so consciously; the patient was sufficiently aware of what had taken place, since he added that he supposed that Dr Penfield was doing something in his brain that caused the movement of his arm. Dr Penfield then asked the patient to stop the movement of his arm, while he continued to stimulate the patient's brain at exactly the same spot. The result: the arm stopped moving! Then Dr Penfield asked the patient to move his right arm while he continued to give a stimulus to the left arm. The patient managed to do exactly as asked! Penfield concluded that yes, the brain gives commands to the body, but apparently something of 'a higher order' was able to 'overrule the brain.' That higher order is what Dr Penfield called the Soul.

I liked that practical approach, but it still left too many questions. Then I found a blog post under the title '*Body, Mind and Soul: a practical approach.*' I quote: 'It would be hard to find three associated words that have caused more confusion than the words 'Body, Mind and Soul.' (…) We prefer practical descriptions over perfect theories, so let us try to express what we need to understand better about the meaning of these three words.

'The essential difference: our body has three dimensions: length, width and height. It is even better to say that our body has four dimensions, adding 'time' as the fourth. In other words: our body has a different shape, over time.

'The contents of our mind, such as thoughts and feelings, of course are lacking the first three dimensions: there is no such thing as a thought of 2×3×1 meters. But thoughts, feelings and so on change over time, almost every second; hence, they show the dimension 'time.'

'And our soul? We prefer to qualify the soul as our 'unchanging essence,' that which does not change over time. At the moment I write these words, I am 59; a lot has changed in my life since I was 19, my body and my mind, but I know deep inside that I am still the same person... The unchangeable quality that 'makes' me 'me,' that is what I call my Soul. Since my Soul does not change, it doesn't show the dimension 'time.' And I don't think I have to argue that my Soul has no physical dimensions either.

'So the Body has four dimensions (length, width, height and time), the Mind only one (time) and the Soul none at all. From that perspective it makes sense not to see ourselves as a Body that has a Mind and a Soul, but just the other way round:

We are Souls that 'have' a Body and a Mind

'With these insights we are ready to draft some useful descriptions:

- My Body is the miraculous, ever changing physical carrier and expression of my Soul, the real Me.
- My Mind is the miraculous, ever changing totality of all the non-physical processes, both conscious as well as unconscious.
- My Soul is the unchangeable quality that makes me the part of the Universe that I really am.'

(End of quote)

Dr Penfield's experiments made likely that there is a 'higher order' than just our brain, which he called the Soul. The quoted blog post made me realize that my Soul is the never-changing essence of who I really am... That vision makes a lot of sense to me. It leaves the question open of what will happen to our soul after death, but to be honest I am not so much interested in that question at the moment: the most important question is what I do as long as I live!

This reminded me of an interview with 'Freddie' Heineken (yes, the man of the great beer) not very long before he died. He was asked if he worried about a life after a death. He instantly answered: '*Not at all. I did not have a problem before I was born, so I will not have a problem after dying either...*' I decided to adopt this very spiritual thought after I heard it the first time...

RENEWED INSPIRATION...

My diving into these few titles in the notebook took me a lot of time, but the result was inspiring. Life was far more flexible and powerful than I ever had thought, on all levels. Synchronizing with the ever present source of life is possible on all levels of existence. The new insights may not provide me with *certainty*, but undoubtedly will tremendously increase the *likelihood* of living a great life.

I promised myself never to lose all that inspiring insight again.

'Grant that I may be beautiful inside.

Let all my external possessions

be in friendly harmony with what is within.'

Socrates

PERSONALITY MATTERS!

DON'T GIVE UP, JUST CHANGE DIRECTION...

Originally I thought this title was just meant as an encouragement. But one way or the other, these words came back to me over and over again. So I decided to just google these words as well. The result was disappointing: a quite confusing series of 'self help' web sites of, to say the least, mixed quality. The words 'Don't give up' prompted me to have another try. This time I googled the sentence between double quotation marks: *"Don't give up, just change direction."* Using double quotation marks instructs the Google Search Engine to look for this exact wording or phrase. That produced totally different results: at the top of the results list I read *'The Cats Turn Around and Start again Lyrics.'* When I clicked it, a poem—the song lyric— opened that touched my heart really deeply... Here it is:

Turn Around and Start Again

So you say your world is falling down around your ears

Everything you've planned has gone astray through all the years

Lift your head my friend, try to see the other thing

Don't give up, just change direction

Turn around and start again

-o-o-o-

Was a time when I was down with not a penny to my name

And like you I was in mind to throw away my chance of fame

Dry your tears as I did then, disregard the falling rain

Don't give up, just change direction

Turn around and start again

-o-o-o-

So spend an hour in meditation, see the good things, not the bad

And you'll find that life has given you good reason to be glad

While the spark remains you must try and try again

Don't give up, just change direction

Turn around and start again

-o-o-o-

Yes, for the world is full of people

With their hope and future gone

They were faced with your decision

To give up or to go on

-o-o-o-

While the spark remains you must try and try again

Don't give up, just change direction

Turn around and start again

These words could have been written just for me. But they weren't: the lyrics are of a 1968 song by *The Cats*, a Dutch rock band. To hear the song yourself, go to www.youtube.com and search there for 'turn around and start again'; it will be there near the top of the results. Listening to the song while reading the words is highly recommended. If you are reading this book at a time when your life is, as mine was until quite recently, not that easy, this old song may touch your heart and encourage you a lot. As it did me!

The next title in the notebook was:

KNOW THYSELF

Under this title was written:

Get your Personal Scan before reading on!

www.ThePersonalScan.com

It was the only reference to any website made in the notebook. So, of course, I opened that site instantly. It is packed with inspiring knowledge, insights, wisdom and practical tips. *However: don't read too much of it!* That is to say: don't read too much before getting your own Personal Scan first.

I soon understood the reason for this warning: The Personal Scan is a Personality Report based on an online questionnaire you are asked to complete; 60 simple questions you can answer in about 15 minutes. When you know too much about the underlying psychological theory, this knowledge might influence the way you answer the 60 questions and thereby the outcome of your Personal Scan Report; therefore it's better to get your Personal Scan first. For the same reason it is recommended not to read the remaining parts of this chapter before getting your Personal Scan.

So of course I bought my Personal Scan instantly. Bought, since it is not free, although in my opinion The Personal Scan is cheap for the many deep and practical insights it brings. A very nice feature on the Personal Scan website, however, is that you can complete your questionnaire, store the results and get a first indication about your Personality Type, all free of charge; later on you can buy the full reports if you want.

So even if you don't want to buy your Personal Scan now for whatever reason, it is highly recommended to complete the online Questionnaire anyway; that's free without any obligations. Just start by clicking 'Get your Scan' in the upper right part of almost every page of the site *thepersonalscan.com.*

I liked my Personal Scan Report a lot, a feeling I share, as I discovered later on, with about 95% of the users so far. Amazing—even almost shocking—that such an accurate description of a personality can come from only 60 simple questions! More about the Personal Scan in the next parts of this chapter.

But first I want to pay some more attention to the title of this part: *'Know Thyself.'* These two words have had a long history. They were originally written, as far as we know, centuries before Christ above the entry door to the temple of Apollo in Delphi, Greece. Not in English of course but in the ancient Greek language: *Gnothi Seauton*. Delphi was the site of the Delphic oracle, the most important oracle in the classical Greek world.

Although oracles may seem a bit weird through our 21st century eyes, they were definitely not in the past: oracles were consulted for centuries in the search for wisdom in important decisions by almost everyone, from kings, philosophers and athletes to the common man. To be honest, many types of prophecies are still used in our time as well, from astrology and the I Ching through weather forecasts and health predictions, and so on.

Apollo was in ancient Greece the God of inspiration, the light and the sun, truth and prophecy; and he had connections with medicine and healing, music, poetry, the arts and the sports... So, a very important God, which no doubt contributed to the echoing of the two words above the door of his temple through all ages.

Socrates, one of the most famous ancient philosophers, was known for his constant emphasis on the tremendous importance of knowing oneself; it was his 'leading theme,' not only in his philosophy and teaching but also in the way he lived and even died.

Much closer to our own time is the poem *Gnothi Seauton* (Know Thyself) of Ralph Waldo Emerson,-(1803–1882) still regarded as one of the grand masters of American poetry. The essence of that poem is that humans are a spark of God without, most of the time, realizing it.

And now these two words had turned up in 'my' notebook! Reading through some of the 104,000 results Google presented from the search of 'Know Thyself,' I suddenly felt quite startled when I discovered, that these two words are only the opening of a full sentence, that reads:

> *'Know thyself*
> *and thou shalt know all the mysteries*
> *of the Gods and the Universe.'*

Wow...! Would knowing oneself really be *that* important? At the moment I read this whole sentence for the first time, I had a very

strange experience: on one hand I was surprised and a bit...
shall I phrase it... 'suspicious' about the tremendous importance ᴛ
sentence seemed to give to the capacity to know oneself. On the other
hand something deep inside me 'knew' that this sentence hit the nail
on the head of life's reality...

And I have to confess: the more I started learning about myself, the
more I started to understand others. The more I started to understand
others, the stronger my relations with people became, both in private
life and in work. These increasingly strong relationships grew my self-
confidence, which made me prosper in every aspect of life. It only
happened over time of course. *But... it happened to me as it can happen to
you. No doubt about that.*

Enough of this subject. Let's move on to the next title in the notebook
(as you may find out, I quote in the remainder of this chapter substantially from www.ThePersonalScan.com):

You are not your Personality Type!

No single Personality Type in the world describes 'The Real You,'
simply because you are unique!

But that doesn't mean you don't share characteristics with millions of
others. You might be right handed, for example, a physical attribute
one shares with about 80% of the world's population.

Our mind shows such measurable attributes as well. Both physicians
and philosophers have described Personality Types since the days
of ancient Greek philosophers. Psychology is still a quite young
science and it took until the early 20th century before the essence
of psychological types was clearly defined in the work of the world
famous psychologist *Dr Carl Gustav Jung.* His book *Psychological Types*
(1921) was, is, and will continue to be the basis of millions and millions
of psychological assessments and scans made every year all over the
globe. *What Einstein was for physics, Jung was for psychology.* Both men
lived and worked in Zurich (Switzerland) and elsewhere, met several
times and inspired each other quite a bit.

Jung never had the intention of creating a systematic approach for Psychological Types, but years of careful observation made the recognition of common mental characteristics almost unavoidable. Jung's own words are printed on the cover of *Psychological Types*: this book is said to be *"the fruit of nearly twenty years' work in the domain of practical psychology. (…) I came across the problem of Types, for it is one's Psychological Type which (…) determines and limits a person's judgment. My book, therefore, was an effort to deal with the relationship of the individual to the world, to people and things."*

Having even a basic understanding of psychological types, therefore, can have a profound impact on the quality of one's life by improving self-confidence, emotional balance, relationships, learning, work, health and wealth. You *are* not your Personality Type, but no doubt you *have* one…

Jung's work is at the heart of many, if not most, Personality Assessments available today. However, most of them are not based on Jung's original work, but on interpretations of it; or even interpretations of interpretations. I was glad to learn that The Personal Scan is not only based on Jung's original work, but also on recent research about it that brought essential new insights into the essence of Jung's *Personality Types*.

PERSONALITY, IQ AND TALENTS

The human mind is no computer. But what our minds actually *do*—the *functions* of our mind—can be understood more readily by comparing them with the way computers behave.

Please understand the subtle difference: we don't compare the mind with a computer, but only compare *mental processes* with *computer processes*. Two good reasons for this comparison:

• As you will learn in this chapter, a lot of mental processes are in essence quite similar to computer processes. For example, our brain is located in a totally dark place, the skull, and receives input from outside, through our senses. The internal memory of a computer is located in a totally dark place as well and relies on input from outside as well. So we can easily compare the input process of our brain with the input process of a computer.

- Most of us are quite familiar with computers nowadays and comparing our mental processes with those of a computer might help to make the complexity of the brain easier to understand.

Our mind fulfills an impressive series of functions; the most essential Mental Functions are:

1. *input*: how we get input
2. *processing*: how we process information
3. *storage*: how we store information
4. *retrieval*: how we remember information
5. *focus*: how we interact
6. *output*: how we create
7. *learning*: how we change

The functions 3, 4 and 7 (*storage*, *retrieval* and *learning*) are part of 'intelligence' as defined in many IQ tests. IQ is not part of the Personal Scan and will consequently not be described here.

The essence of one's Personality is defined by the other four: *input*, *processing*, *focus* and *output*. Personality has a substantial impact on each aspect of our personal and professional life, including the best way to learn.

Talent can be defined as *'the innate ability to develop a specific competence or skill,'* which is of course something different.

Summarizing:

- *Personality* is about Character,
- *IQ* about Intelligence and
- *Talent* about competences or skills.

Personality, IQ and talents together can tell us a lot—but not all!—about any person. The importance of IQ and talents has been highly overvalued in recent centuries, as Personality has been undervalued. In this chapter we focus mainly on Personality, since a deeper understanding about Personality—both ours and that of others—has a huge impact on our Quality of Life.

1. HOW WE GET INPUT

Our mind gets input by Sensing *and by* Intuition.
All of us have an innate preference for one of these two.

This is the first of four *'Jung Essentials'* I will describe in this part and the following three numbered parts of this chapter.

One of the reasons I really like Jung's work is that he offers 'crispy clear' definitions, to start with Sensing and Intuition

- *Sensing* is defined as mental input through our five senses (seeing, hearing, smell, taste and touch).
- *Intuition* is defined as *any* way of mental input that is not through our senses.

Let's explore Intuition a little further. Getting an idea, for example, is intuitive input into our mind: the trigger for the idea might come through your senses, but the actual getting of that idea is definitely not through your senses, and therefore it's intuitive, by Jung's definition. Suppose a hundred people see the same movie, and three get an idea from seeing it (but each of them a different idea); this illustrates that the actual seeing of the movie was something different from the getting of that idea.

Other kinds of intuitive mental input are: associating different things… seeing patterns and developments… sudden insight in how things correlate… innovative solutions… a paradigm shift… and so on. And last but not least, placing things in time… We can perceive the changes on a clock, but we cannot directly perceive time itself by our senses; so understanding history, envisioning the future, making plans, it's all loaded with intuitive mental input.

Intuition is also getting mental input across the boundaries of time and distance: you suddenly think about a friend you have not seen or heard from for years, and the same day he phones… or you and your friend start to say the same thing at the same moment… or the phone rings and you instantly know who is calling… and so on, and so on.

So, there is a substantial difference between Sensing and Intuition. Since each of us has a preference for either Sensory input or Intuitive input we can distinguish Sensing Types (people with an innate preference for sensory input above intuitive input) from Intuitive Types (the other way around).

- *Sensing Types* are, often literally, 'down to earth' realists, and have a good eye for details. They will prefer concrete things over abstract ones, are quite factual, and concentrate on the here and now.
- *Intuitive Types* have a less developed eye for details, but easily see 'the big picture.' They enjoy abstract things and ideas, are interested in the history of things, and the future, and they recognize opportunities.

An overview:

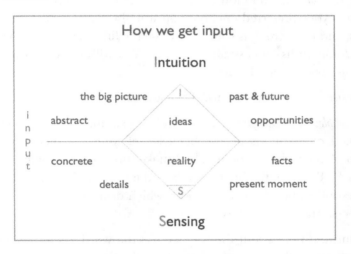

However, Jung did not see these two ways of input as either/or. Quite the reverse; *all of us use both forms of mental input*, but one of them is just better developed than the other. Jung compares it with being left-handed: actually we are 'both-handed' but we have an innate prefer-ence for one of them. The degree of preference differs from person to person: some people do everything with the left hand, while in oth-ers left and right are more equally developed. If the total 'usability' or function of both arms is, normally, 100%, the left hand/right hand balance can be 55%-45% for one person but 90%-10% for another. This last individual, as Jung would say, showed a greater 'differentiation in function.'

With Sensing and Intuition it's exactly the same: together they are 100% of the mental input (thanks to Jung's practical definition of Intuition as "every input in our mind that is not through our senses"); Sensing Types rely more than 50% on their Sensory input, and Intuitive Types more than 50% on Intuitive input. About 70% of all people rely more on Sensing (Sensing Types), and, of course, it follows that the remainder, about 30%, are more reliant on Intuition (Intuitive Types). Since all of us use both forms of mental input, there are no 100% Sensing Types, nor 100% Intuitive Types; however, the preferences for one of these two has a substantial impact on a person's Personality.

Your *Personal Scan* will show not only which of the two types of mental input is your preferred one, but you will also learn how strong your '*S*' is, and how strong is your '*I*' (we use the first character of *S*ensing and *I*ntuition as an easy abbreviation). You will find out how much stronger one is than the other.

How useful are these insights? They are *crucial*!

An example: Let's say you want to hire, for example, someone to make detailed observations of the behavior of your customers in your chain of retail shops: you had best make sure you hire someone with 'high *S*.' But also, the higher the S is, the less comfortable—and less successful—a person will be in jobs which deal mainly with abstract subjects. And so on and so forth.

To finish, a note about the way we use the word 'innate' when we talk about an 'innate preference.' Literally 'innate' means what we started with, at the moment of birth. Of course it is very hard, if not impossible, to make a sharp distinction between what was truly innate and what we learned in our very first years. Science struggles with that as well. But actually the difference is not that important. Both the innate, and the very early (1-2 years) developed mental qualities will scarcely change during our lifetime, and are just an essential, unchangeable part of our being, of our 'core.' It is exactly the total of unchangeable 'core qualities' of a Personality that is visualized in *The Personal Scan Core Profile*, the very first and most essential of all profiles in The Personal Scan's 'family' of scans or profiles.

2. How we process information

Our mind processes all mental input by Thinking *and by* Feeling.
All of us have an innate preference for one of these two.

This is the second of the 'Jung Essentials.'

- *Thinking* is defined as a *logical, objective* way of processing information and uses mostly language. *Thinking tells us 'what anything is.'*
- *Feeling* is defined as giving *personal, subjective* meaning and significance to information. *Feeling tells us 'what anything means for me.'*

This definition of the word 'Feeling' is substantially different from how we use it in everyday language. Thinking and Feeling are in Jung's view the two ways in which we process *all* the input that we get through Senses and Intuition. In other words: Thinking and Feeling are the way we create order in our mind... Both are needed for making that information ready for future use.

An example: In my youth I was once bitten by a Dalmatian and I can assure you that an experience like that made quite a strong mental input. I am 42 years old at the moment but I still don't *like* Dalmatians (Feeling). I *know* (Thinking) of course that Dalmatians are great dogs that normally don't bite any more often than other dogs, but I stay alert as soon as I see them. It's a perfect example how logical information (Thinking) can differ from the personal meaning (Feeling) it has. My encounter with that Dalmatian was made ready for future reference by adding an 'alarm label' to it that pops up in my mind every time I see a dog that even looks like one of that breed. Much later I learned that not all Dalmatians are dangerous, and a second label—good dog—was added to the same word, a Thinking one this time. As a result Dalmatians will still alarm me, but *my logical mind helps me to handle it and to balance the feeling.*

In the same way all mental input we receive is either ignored or will be made ready for future reference by adding Thinking and Feeling 'labels' to it. (A note: this process of labeling information is exactly the same as what was written earlier about *How we create meaning* in the sub chapter *Your Miraculous Brain*).

As is the case with Sensing and Intuition each of us has an innate preference for one of these two ways to process information.

An overview:

- *Thinking Types* prefer the objective, rational way to order mental input, like norms, definitions, rules, laws, standards, systems and procedures.

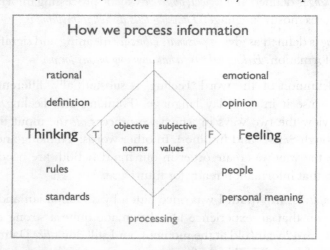

- *Feeling types*, by contrast, prefer the more subjective and emotional way to order mental input: personal experiences, emotions, opinions, values, prejudices and so on. Prejudices often do decide what any mental input means for us.

We use the character 'T' for Thinking and 'F' for Feeling as abbreviations.

Please note: *we 'label' people in exactly the same way.* We may, for example, continue to deal with a person we don't like (Feeling) just because he is a good customer (Thinking). Or someone can still love (Feeling) someone else with a very bad history (Thinking). When falling in love, the Feeling can be so strong that we ignore almost all rational arguments about the one we love, which is well illustrated in the proverb 'Love is blind.'

The great Dutch philosopher Dr Arnold Cornelis taught us a lot more about how feeling actually works in his intriguing book *The Logic of Feeling.* His work and insights are embedded in The Personal Scan as well.

The *Big Four* is a name used to describe the 4 functions of the mind, we have seen so far : the 2 ways to get mental *input*—by *Sensing* and *Intuition*—and the 2 ways to *process* that input—by *Thinking* and *Feeling.* These Big Four are of crucial importance since they stand at the very beginning of our consciousness. Recent Brain Research proved that each of these Big Four Mental Functions is located in a different part of the brain, which, after almost a century, adds an other layer of scientific proof to Jung's crucial insights in the human mind.

3. HOW WE INTERACT

Our mind interacts with the outside world by Adapting *and* Reflecting. *All of us have an innate preference for one of these two.*

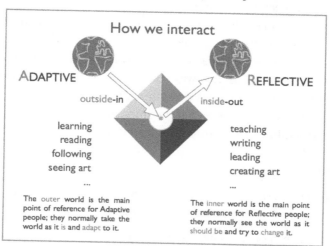

This is the third of our 'Jung Essentials.' Jung called these two ways to interact with the outside world *Mental Attitudes.*

- The *outer* world is the main point of reference for *Adaptive Types*; they normally take the outside world *as it is* and *adapt* to it.

- The *inner* world is the main point of reference for *Reflective Types*: they normally see the outside world *as it could be, or even should be* and try to *change* it.

Adaptive Types (A) and Reflective (R) behavior is so common that we are most of the time completely unaware of it. *Learning* is an *outside-in-movement* and therefore Adaptive, whereas *teaching* is an *inside-out* movement and therefore Reflective. In the same way *reading* is Adaptive and writing Reflective, while leading is Reflective and *following* Adaptive. We could easily expand this list… almost endlessly.

It is important to realize that the Adaptive and Reflective attitudes can be combined with each of the Big Four Mental Functions we have seen so far. A land surveyor, for example, uses his Sensing function mostly outside-in (Adaptive Sensing), while a designer uses the Senses mostly inside-out (Reflective Sensing). We could easily find such examples for the other Mental Functions as well.

One more aspect to mention here: both Adaptive and Reflective behaviors are normally focused on specific 'objects': people, jobs, houses, money, and so on. *In other words, the Adaptive Preference does not mean that we adapt to everything, but mainly to the people and things we have chosen to be important for us.* Likewise, the Reflective Preference does not mean that we try to influence everything, but mainly, again, the people and things we have chosen to be important for us. Consequently the two Mental Attitudes are also referred to as *Focus*, or *Orientation*.

4. HOW WE CREATE OUTPUT

> *Our mind creates output by iMprovising and by sYstematic behavior.*
> *All of us have an innate preference for one of these two.*

This is the fourth of the 'Jung Essentials.' However, it has to be said that Jung described these two ways to create output or, if you prefer, to organize our life, only indirectly. The difference is based on our two brain halves.

- The *left half* of our brain (or just: the Left Brain) uses mostly *language* and *logic* for its processes
- the right half of the brain (or just: the Right Brain) relies more on whole *impressions* like pictures, music, smells etc

The Left Brain can only handle a few inputs at a time (as you are doing right now, reading one word at a time), while the Right Brain is able to see a whole picture at once. For the computer savvy: Dr Jill Bolte Taylor compared the Left Brain with a *serial processor*, that can only process a thing after completing the previous one, and the Right Brain with a *'parallel processor'*, that can process many things at the same time. To illustrate the difference: whenever you need lights for the Christmas tree, you'd better buy lights which are wired in *parallel*, since in a *serial* ordered cord of lights all lights will go out whenever one light fails.

The difference between these two brain halves in everyday life is huge. Take for example getting driving lessons. At the beginning one has to think of all the different instructions: if you correctly remember the first three instructions, you forget the fourth; so you concentrate on the fourth and suddenly forget the third. But after sufficient lessons and practice, you don't even have to think at all any longer: you just get behind the wheel of your car and drive away.

That is exactly how we normally learn: most learning starts in the serial, step-by-step Left Brain and is only completed when the parallel, more holistic Right Brain has taken over. During our initial lessons we have to think and concentrate so much that it is hard to improvise; but once the Right Brain has taken over, improvising is so easy that we often don't even realize we're doing it.

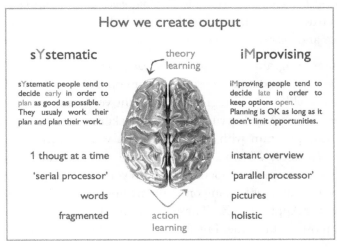

How we create output

sYstematic	theory learning	iMprovising
sYstematic people tend to decide early in order to plan as good as possible. They usualy work their plan and plan their work.		iMproving people tend to decide late in order to keep options open. Planning is OK as long as it doen't limit opportunities.
1 thougt at a time		instant overview
'serial processor'		'parallel processor'
words		pictures
fragmented	action learning	holistic

In other words: the Left Brain is more step-by-step and *systematic*, while the Right Brain is more holistic and *improvising*. In The Personal Scan we use the words *sYstematic* and *iMprovising* as the key words to describe these two totally different mental processes. As you see, the second character of sYstematic and iMprovising is a capital letter used as an abbreviation; the first characters of these words, S and I, are not available since these are already used for Sensing and Intuition.

And again, every one of us has an innate preference for one of these two mental output functions.

- *sYstematic Types* tend to decide early and normally plan their work and work their plan.

- *iMprovising Types* tend to decide as late as possible in order to keep all options open for future input.

THE 2 LEVELS OF THE MIND

Our mind operates on two levels: Conscious and SubConscious.
The role of the subconscious mind is
to help overcome the limitations of consciousness mind.

This is the fifth of the 'Jung Essentials.'

I wrote before, in 'Your miraculous raw material': *"Reality' is always composed of two levels: the level we can experience and the level we can't experience.'* That is true for our mind as well. Our mind functions on two levels: *Conscious* and *Subconscious*. The first cannot exist without the second…

Computer programs can run in the *foreground* or in the *background*. When you are reading a website on your computer for example, that website is visible in the foreground, but at the very same moment there are at least two programs running in the background: your computer's *browser* (the program with which you open websites, most probably Internet Explorer, Firefox, Google Chrome or Safari) and its *operating system* (the program that opens and closes your computer—and organizes everything that is going on in the meantime—such as Microsoft Windows or Apple's OS X). These background programs are invisible to you most of the time, but they are nevertheless crucial for each good working computer. The foreground and background programs are the two essential levels of any computer, PDA (personal digital assistant), smartphone and the like.

The human mind has such a foreground and background as well. The foreground is our *Consciousness* or *Conscious Mind*. It's our Conscious Mind that experiences input from our five senses, that allows us to think, to experience emotions, to make choices and so on. Our Conscious Mind is so often 'in the foreground' of everything, that we tend to ignore the other part of our brain: the Subconscious Mind.

But it's the *Subconscious Mind* that regulates almost all of the processes in our body; if we had to consciously regulate all those processes we'd have absolutely no brainpower left to do anything else. Our Subconscious is also the 'space' in which almost all our memories are stored. Most of the time we are not aware of our memories, unless there is a 'trigger' to make us dig them up from our memory-warehouse. If we meet old friends, for example, a good chat can bring back memories we've not been aware of for many, many years. Hypnosis can also bring memories back, with an astonishing amount of detail.

One more example: often, when we forget a name, try as we may, we just can't find it. Yet as soon as we stop the conscious attempt to find that name the Subconscious Mind takes over: while we use our Conscious Mind in the foreground—for example, to continue the story we were telling—the Subconscious Mind keeps running in the background until it has found that name. Very often that name will then 'pop up' in the midst of a sentence of our story and we will interrupt ourselves with an 'Oh… I remember his name: it was Phil Brady.'

Jung taught that the Subconscious Mind tries to compensate and complete our Conscious Attitude. That sounds difficult but it's not that hard at all: it just means that if we for example, are over-adapting to the outside world, we neglect our inner world; our Subconscious Mind will try to compensate for that by giving a series of signals. Gentle signals to start with, and then stronger ones if we neglect the softer kind! Such an increasing series of emotions will normally be accompanied by physical reactions as well.

An example: Steve, a police officer, worked way too hard, not only because he was very involved in his work but also because of his boss pushing for results much too early. Moreover, his wife and kids claimed his attention quite a lot as well, which he totally understood; yet at times he experienced it as being unreasonable.

At first, Steve felt just a bit uncomfortable with his whole situation, but then later on he felt a little irritated; and next, really irritated, followed by becoming angry at almost everyone, yet still without expressing his feelings. His health deteriorated considerably during that period and he slowly became aware that he should visit a doctor. But he didn't...

One day it all became just too much. The day started with a 'stupid' argument with his spouse, which meant that he could not get the children to school on time. At the Police Office he was greeted by his boss, who blamed him for the angry phone call he'd just had from the mayor about a still unsolved murder which had received plenty of unwelcome publicity. Then it happened: Steve's subconscious compensated for Steve's too long adaptation to the expectations of others and Steve exploded in uncontrollable, unreasonable, angry behavior, much to his own surprise! He told off his boss and in the presence of all his colleagues announced his resignation; then he stomped out of the office and slammed the door as hard as he could. His wife got more or less the same treatment, after which Steve went to the bedroom, locked the door and stayed there for hours, heavily depressed and often in tears while feeling a lot of pain in his body.

Luckily this story had a happy end: Steve visited his doctor, who was wise enough not to put Steve on all kinds of medicines; he just explained to Steve what had happened, and Steve recognized instantly the truth of what the doctor was saying. He went home, had a good and long talk with his wife, phoned his boss who not only understood what happened but also had recognized his own role in the story from some talks with Steve's colleagues. Steve and his boss had a good talk the next day, after which Steve took almost two weeks off, and successfully changed some of his habits...

So far this story. Stories like Steve's happen millions of times every day, and they happen all over the world. Unfortunately not all have a happy ending... Understanding the compensating nature of the Subconscious Mind and learning to 'hear' its signals quite early would make the lives of most people much happier.

Consciousness and subconsciousness[1] ... together they make 'our world turn.' When we compare them with an iceberg, our Consciousness is the part that's above the water... I feel as if I have only scratched the surface of this subject. And no doubt that's true. But this is what I can share here.

THE 4 NATURES

Our innate preference for Sensing or Intuition and for Thinking or Feeling leads to 4 combinations, the 4 Natures, that are the basis of our mind.

This is the sixth of the 'Jung Essentials.'

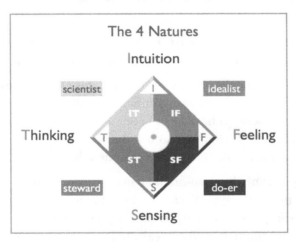

When we are born, only two of these Basic Functions are active: Sensing and Feeling. In our very first years we get a tremendous amount of mental input through our senses and can only order that by Feeling.

---

[1] Subconsciousness is often called 'unconsciousness' by scientists, Jung included.

These two basic functions together are characterized as belonging to the *Do-er* (S+F: *Sensing Feelers*).

Normally our parents start to teach us their language and almost all parents start with the words 'mama' and 'papa' or the equivalents in their language. Once these words are said to us several hundred times we have learned both the words and what they mean. The learning of the whole language proceeds in exactly the same way and over time goes even faster. With language the *Sensing Thinker* (S+T) in us has arrived; and for him we coined the term, the *'Steward.'*

Until this stage of our childhood, learning was mostly about concrete three-dimensional 'things.' It normally takes between four and six years before children start to understand abstract notions and get a sense of time; and of mortality. This understanding is actually the end of the first phase of childhood. Abstract input to our minds cannot take place through our senses, and is therefore by definition Intuitive. The *Intuitive Thinker* (I+T) in us has come to the stage, characterized by the word *Scientist*.

Last but not least the Intuitive Feeler is 'born,' one who combines Intuition with Feeling (I+F). We have termed this the Idealist.

Note: The names Idealist, Scientist, Steward and Do-er are oversimplified names for the related four combinations of Basic Mental Functions. It would perhaps have been better not to use any word and just mention 'Intuitive Feeler' and so on. But that could make more difficult a deeper understanding—and yes, there is more coming!

All four quadrants have substantial significance, as have the colors used both in the Personal Scan logo as in the icons: the green of the earth (Steward), the blue of water (Do-er), the yellow of the sunny sky (Scientist) and the red of fire (Idealist). They also represent the four states of anything in nature: in the same order solid (green), liquid (blue), gas (yellow) and energy (red).

Jung discovered that each of us has an innate preference for one Input and one Processing function. Therefore we all have an innate preference for one of the four combinations, for which we have coined the term *The Four Natures*.

A short characterisation of each of these Four Natures:

The Do-ers (SF—blue—30% of the population)

As the name suggests, Do-ers love action, experience and adventure. As Sensing persons they have a great eye for detail, are practical and prefer the physical, concrete things above the abstracts. As Feelers, they are more attracted to people than to systems. Personal values and meaning are more important to them than formal standards and norms.

The Stewards (ST—green—40% of the population)

In dictionaries a Steward is often defined as 'A person who takes responsibility to care (for something)' and that is the core of the ST (Sensing + Thinking) nature. As Sensing persons they have a great eye for detail, are practical and prefer the physical, concrete things above the abstracts. As Thinkers, they always try to be reasonable and they like to use systems, procedures, definitions, norms and standards; they're more attracted to people than to systems.

The Scientists (IT—yellow—20% of the population)

Scientist love to raise questions and to go after the answers. As Thinkers, they want to be as objective as possible, and of course they need some framework, methods, rules and procedures. Their Intuitive nature has a preference for abstract 'things' above the physical ones as they prefer opportunities over security. As soon as an answer is found on the question at hand, they move on to the next object of their interest.

The Idealists (IF—red—10% of the population)

While the Scientist is more attracted to *knowing*, the Idealist is more a *believer*; the scientist knows by *brains*, the idealist knows by *heart*. His Intuitive nature is attracted to abstractions as well, but the combination with Feeling focuses the idealism more on people than on knowledge. Personal values, freedom, respect, serving and faith are his 'daily food.'

Practical use:

Although the above is still a very, very rough first description of the nature of the different Personalities, it may be clear that the difference in Nature gives substantial insight. If you want to hire a priest, an artist, an accountant or a professor, the Four Natures would definitely give you a first impression. In marketing, each Nature is a quite different target group and needs different messages in communication.

THE 8 MAIN PERSONALITY TYPES

One of the Big Four Mental Functions
(Sensing, Intuition, Thinking and Feeling) is Dominant.

In other words, one of the Big Four Mental Functions is stronger than all others and dominates the personality. This is the seventh of the 'Jung Essentials.' As a consequence, each of the Four Natures comes 'in two flavors' as shown in the next picture. Each Steward, for example, can either be a *Sensing Steward* (in case Sensing is the Dominant Function) or a *Thinking Steward* (in case Thinking is dominant).

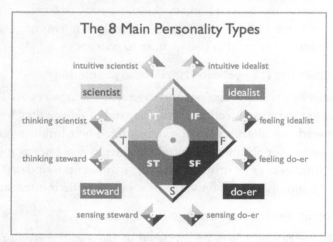

An example: Fred and Steve, who are both Police Officers. It would be no surprise to find that both are 'Steward' in their Personal Scan. However Fred as a *Sensing Steward* is more attracted to 'hands on' police work on the streets, while Steve as a *Thinking Steward* prefers the Criminal Research which requires more fact finding and analysis.

Although Jung 'invented' the Dominant Mental Function, he did not describe how to determine which of the Big Four Mental Functions is the Dominant one. The Personal Scan uses a quite complex algorithm to determine the Dominant Mental Function, which goes beyond the scope of this book.

As you might have noticed in the picture, each of the Eight Main Personality Types has its own Icon or 'Diamond' that is derived from the Personal Scan logo.

With a bit of practice one can learn to 'read' these 8 Main Personality Icons and to understand the main characteristics of a person directly from his or her Personality Icon. These Icons can be ideal for any kind of team-building and even conflict solving.

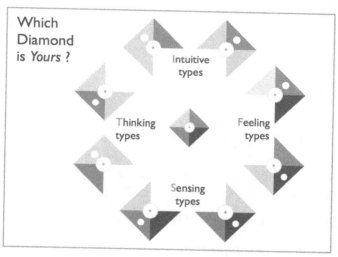

Which Diamond is Yours ?

Intuitive types

Thinking types

Feeling types

Sensing types

Although the knowledge behind all the above has been drawn directly and 100% from Jung's essential teachings, the above interpretation and nomenclature is a unique and new discovery derived from Jung's work, as is its consistent visualization in the icons.

32 PERSONALITY TYPES

The seven 'Jung essentials' define 32 different Personality Types: 4×2×2×2.

This is not another 'Jung Essential,' but simply the consequences of the seven essentials described under the seven subheadings which we've examined.

Your Personality Type is, like that of anyone else, mainly defined by your innate preference for:

- *Input*: Sensing and Intuition (S and I)
- *Processing*: Thinking and Feeling (T and F)
- *Attitude*: Adaptive and Reflective (A and R)
- *Output*: sYstematic and iMprovising (Y and M)

The *Personal Scan Assessment*, 60 simple questions, results in the Personality Graph, which makes visible your preference on each of the four axes, as well as the strength of each preference. The Personality Reports contain far more information: several more graphs, your Personality Description, your Personality Pincode and your Personality Icon. A solid introduction to the theory behind the Scan is presented, as well as recommendations for applying the Personal Scan to living a great life.

Please note: the sum of all preferences is for $4 \times 100\% = 400\%$. Always. For everybody. *No one is less or more* than anyone else; nevertheless, *we are all different* by virtue of our Mental Preferences, and also by the strength of each axis (for example 80% − 20% is a different strength than 55% − 45%, even when both equal 100%).

The above results in thirty two (32) Personality Types:

- The preference for Input (S or I) and Processing (T or F) result in $2 \times 2 = 4$ combinations, called *The Four Natures*.
- One function in each Nature is *Dominant*, which makes that every Nature comes 'in two flavors,' resulting in $4 \times 2 = 8$ Main Personality Types.
- Combining these eight with the preference for one of the two Mental Attitudes (A or R) results in $8 \times 2 = 16$ combinations.

Combining these sixteen with the preference for one of the two Brain Halves (Y or M) brings us finally to $16 \times 2 = 32$ Personality Types, each of which is represented by a different Personality Icon, all based on the 8 Main Personality Icons mentioned above.

Sure, the above is a lot of information. And most of it might be new for you as well. I hope you have got your own Personal Scan in the meantime, which makes the above much more relevant to your personal circumstances. With it, you will arrive at a far better understanding of everything—starting with yourself.

Altogether the above is a high quality 'Psychological Tool Box' which is on the one hand quite easy to understand, and on the other hand remarkably powerful.

However... a good carpenter's tool box by itself doesn't make a good carpenter... And a good Mental Tool Box doesn't make us instantly 'better people.' Substantial learning and practice are needed in both cases. Luckily there are courses, lectures, workshops and many other ways to learn more.

LIVING AND WORKING TOGETHER

Just like we all have a personal mind,
teams have a collective Mind and even a collective Personality.

And the smallest team is a personal relation...

Although Jung did not pay special attention to relationships and teams, his work is filled with examples we can use in these fields. I was excited to discover that the Personality Icons as used in The Personal Scan and The Team Scan help a lot to substantially improve both my *personal relations* and my role on several *teams*. No wonder: a profound and deeper understanding of life as given by these tools, will manifest itself on any level of existence.

At this very moment I don't feel 'ready' yet to say much more about it. But no doubt I'll want to dive deeper into this subject later on.

CHANGED FOR THE BETTER...

There's no doubt... Personality matters... a lot!

I didn't know much about Personality and Personality Type before the notebook made me look for it. In the meantime I did not only learn a great amount, the insights also changed the way I interact with people.

That boosted my *self-confidence* and *self-esteem*. The reactions from people around me made me realize that I have changed for the better. Which encourages me to continue, of course. I am still a beginner in this field and I realize I have a lot to learn; so I've registered for several courses in the meantime. For the first time in many years I am looking forward to the future...!

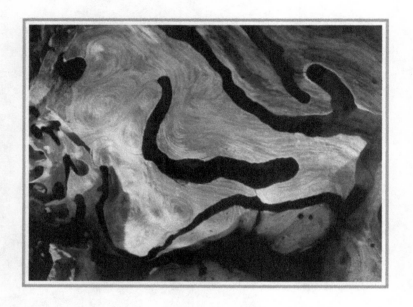

'Few are those who see with their own eyes
and feel with their own hearts.'

Albert Einstein

SURPRISE... SURPRISE...

I had done such a lot in so few weeks... but I wasn't tired. Not at all! I felt energized, inspired and way better than I had felt in many years. Nevertheless I decided to take a break from research and writing for at least my last day on beautiful Salt Spring Island. I had taken small breaks every day during my trip, going for a walk or having a bite in one of the cute restaurants. Salt Spring (the word 'island' is most times left out) has some interesting tag-lines in various media: the Island is referred to as *Organic Capital of Canada*, and *Artists' Paradise*, while the local Tourism Board uses the slogan *Out of the Ordinary*.

All three make perfect sense. Although other places call themselves *Organic Capital* as well, it will be hard to find a community in Northern America that has more organic growers and products than Salt Spring. More than 300 different kinds of organic apples alone are grown on its 74 square miles. The Salt Spring Seeds Sanctuary has grown over 600 varieties of heritage and heirloom organic seeds of vegetables, beans, grains and herbs for more than 24 years, and ships them all over the world. Salt Spring cow and goat cheese is quite famous, as is Salt Spring Coffee and Salt Spring Mussels. No wonder there are special gourmet tours on the island! The island's Apple Festival and Fall Fair are definitely worth a visit, as are many of its other festivals.

The name *Artists' Paradise* suits the island well; hundreds of artists live on Salt Spring Island: writers, painters, ceramicists, wood turners, spinners, quilters, instrument makers, songwriters, composers, musicians, film makers, photographers, and so on... whatever art you can name, it's likely to be on Salt Spring—and some of the island's artist are famous in Canada and abroad. Don't be surprised to find more than one Salt Spring author on a Canadian Bestseller list at the same time. The arts are visible all over the place: plenty of galleries and studios, a great studio tour, a nice theatre, an Arts Council with its own cute exhibition Hall and even several informal 'art guilds' where the local artists collaborate. The island even has its own Film Festival—amazing for a community of only around ten thousand residents, isn't it?

Both the organic foods and the craftwork and art are sold at Salt Spring's famous open air Market in the Park or Salt Spring Market. Only products that pass the test '*You make it, you bake it, or you grow it*' are allowed to be sold at the market, in which the 'you' is, of course, one of the residents. This rule is as simple as it is powerful: it continues to focus attention on the island's crafts folk and natural growers. I had visited the market this Saturday and enjoyed the market, the products, the sellers, the many tourists, as well as the crisp fresh air and the music in the park's gazebo. The 'Food Alley' adjoining the market, where some great chefs have their restaurants, adds to the fun, as do the other restaurants, several with live music. All things together create a very special atmosphere.

Beyond doubt Salt Spring is *Out of the Ordinary*, as its third tagline says. The only thing that misses mention in all those taglines is the spectacular natural beauty...

I had good memories of Salt Spring from my youth, since it was our family's holiday destination more than once. I was pleasantly surprised that the island had only become better over the years. Substantially more crowded of course, but nevertheless better. More than a hundred B&Bs, some fine hotels and at least one great camping ground—the one on Ruckle Park, overlooking some Gulf Islands and San Juan Islands as viewed directly from your tent!—makes a stay on Salt Spring affordable for any wallet. The ferries are quite expensive, but not if you go as a foot passenger. Flying with the island's 'own' seaplane line, Salt Spring Air, is no doubt a special pleasure because of the great views over all those islands and mountains lying in the silver-blue waters.

RUCKLE PARK

As said before, I took a 'full break' on the last day of the May Long Weekend and went for a long walk in beautiful Ruckle Park. The British Columbia Parks website describes Ruckle as one of the most beautiful parks in the southern Gulf Islands; I quote: '*Pitch your tent in the grassy meadow overlooking Swanson Channel then lie back and relax, watching pleasure boats and ferries sail by in a stately and colorful parade. With its 7 kilometers of shoreline, rocky headlands and tiny coves and bays, Ruckle Park provides hours or even days of enjoyable exploration.*

Close to the camping, on one of the many small capes, is my favorite bench. Sitting on it you don't see anything but the spectacular view over some smaller Canadian Gulf Islands and over the USA's San Juan Islands. You feel surrounded by water…

Around noon, eating my sandwich, I had an impression that someone was looking towards me. I turned around and… big surprise: there stood the Man, no more than 30 metres from my bench! He waved his arm and called: '*Hey man… I thought I recognized you! That's a nice surprise!*'

I waved back, speechless…

With quick, energetic steps the Man walked up to me and we hugged as if we'd been close friends for years. In the same split second I realized that many long-time friends had actually not been real friends at all. And I realized:

*The significance of friendship lies in its depth,
not in its length.*

But I didn't have much time for this insight, because the Man asked: 'What brought you here?' A very nice conversation started, which I report from the notes I made the same day. No doubt our meeting was one of life's synchronicities.

What a good listener that man was! He seemed really interested in me and asked only a few questions, most times to encourage me to tell more. I learned that he was visiting Salt Spring as one of the teachers of a course. When I told him how the notebook had changed my life in only a couple of weeks, his body language showed that he was very happy to hear this, but he just went on listening. At a certain moment he asked me if I had the notebook with me and when I nodded, he asked if he could read it. I handed him the notebook, which was now loaded with my own notes, under the titles and subtitles he originally wrote. I was happy and proud on the one hand, but a little reluctant on the other: what if my notes were not at all in line with what he originally meant with his titles?

He seemed to feel my hesitation, and a big smile came over his face as he said: 'Don't worry. This is not an examination. I only ask it for two reasons: to learn from your experiences and to see how I can encourage you further to keep going.'

Then he started reading… fully concentrated as if he had all the time in the world. He asked a few brief questions when he couldn't read something or wasn't sure what I meant with some things I had written or drawn. He gave no comment at all, and all the time he was reading, his body language was not giving me the slightest idea of what he thought about it. Observing him I learned that people can 'listen' with their whole body while reading…

When he finished reading, he asked courteously for my Personal Scan Report, which I had with me as well, and I handed it to him. He was obviously familiar with these reports since it took only a few minutes before he gave both the notebook and the Scan Report back to me, and only said: 'Just what I thought…' and with hardly a pause he continued: 'Man, you really worked on it, didn't you? I am so glad for you that you've begun to see the miracle that life actually is. Maybe you can't see it yourself, but there are huge differences in your radiance since the first time we met. You were so miserable then and so filled with new hope and energy now!'

Although he had assured me that this was not an examination, I felt as if I just passed one. Now it was my turn to have a big, happy smile on my face. I could almost see it from inside. His simple, warm words lit up my body, mind and soul and were so tremendously encouraging!

'Thank you,' I said with a faltering voice. 'Absolutely my pleasure' he replied, 'Not always does my little trigger book—as I call the almost empty notebook that I give away in very rare cases—perform such a good job. But when it does, as with you, it's double the pleasure.'

'You only give your notebooks in very rare cases, you say??' I replied. 'So why did you give one to me?'

He observed me for a moment, before he said, carefully looking for the right words: 'I gave you it because my intuition told me you were ready for it. You know... no one can teach people anything if they are not ready to learn it. As the proverb says:

'When the chatra is ready, the guru will be there...'

'Where *chatra* is Hindi for 'student' and *guru* stands for 'teacher' or master. Please understand me well: I am not 'a guru' in the western meaning of that word, but being a teacher at the 'University of Life' is actually something I like. Not so long ago I was a quite conventional high school teacher, instructing my students what to read and how to explain everything, with the best intentions by the way. At that time I often gave people advice as well. But over time I learned—the hard way—that instructions, explanations and advice are the wrong tools to really help people improve their quality of life: it's way better just to trigger people to find *their* way, not to come up with *my* way... As I said, I have learned these lessons 'the hard way' since *life's most effective lessons were delivered packed in severe problems*... For example when so-called 'good friends' misused my trust and confidence in them and so-called business 'partners' swindled me; which took me into a depression at least as deep as yours was...'

He paused for a while, looking out over the Salish Sea, deep in thoughts. It gave me some time to recover from my amazement that the Man himself had once been in a deep depression as well. Almost unbelievable... but suddenly I realized that I had more or less made a Saint of him, which he obviously wasn't. At least, I supposed that Saints can't have depressions, or can they? That was a funny thought. Seeing the Man for the first time as the real human being he was, not only made him seem closer to me, but filled me with hope as well: if *he* had been able to grow into the man he was now from the depressed one he had been before, *I* should be able to grow 'a stronger me' as well... Then, abruptly, he came out of his pensive mood, looked intensely at me as if he was reading my mind, and continued:

'I never forgave the people who cheated me. Whatever I tried, I couldn't do it, until one of my masters helped me to discover that

I shouldn't even try to forgive them. *Forgiveness, as we have learned it, is a kind of favor we do to others.* And that is hard when one is deceived and swindled. *'Forgive and forget' is just impossible for the human brain*: there is no way we can get rid of a brain circuit once it is made. But what we can do is re-label our memories... connect our memories to different mental labels...'

'The 'trick' is,' he said, 'to realize that we should not do *them* a favor, but do one for *ourselves*, by getting rid of the destructive energy that we literally keep in our body and mind, for just as long as we keep destructive emotional labels attached to certain memories. You have, I think, learned enough about the brain to understand how we label our experiences. It is *me* who labels my memories, me and nobody else...! *The only difference between a plain fact and a negative fact, is my judgement.* Between being a prisoner of negative emotions from my past and being a free man, stands only one thought, one label! You have learned about the 'count-to-90 rule,' so you know that we *are* able to get rid of negative emotions as rapidly as 90 seconds after such an emotion happens. In about one and a half minutes an emotion is completely flushed out of our body, yet we can stay in the emotion by re-playing the brain circuit, which was created in the meantime, over and over again, as the rats did with the camphor in the brain research. You wrote about in your notes. But... we can also decide to let the negative emotions go.'

He continued, in a convincing tone: 'Since *everything in the past is* just a memory, or even better *an unchangeable memory*, I'd do better to get rid of any negative labels that are counter-productive to my future. I'd be better off letting them go... and had better accept the swindlers as the people they obviously *are*... I should better accept the *facts* as merely the *facts* that happened in *reality*, not those I see in my judging mind. And again: not to do any favor for *them*, but to set *myself* free! I can't forget, but I can remove the negative labels. I can train myself in the mental attitude of 'let it be.'.. Am I clear?,' he said with quite some emphasis.

Oh yes! Without question he was. What he said made so much sense! In my mental eye I saw many people, facts and incidents that I could with benefit discard from a whole series of negative emotions. 'Rip it out!,' an inner voice told me, and I remembered that scene in the movie *Dead Poets Society*, in which Mr Keating, the English teacher, spoke these words to his embarrassed students. Ripping those negative labels out of my personal history, all of them... that is what I decided to do, no matter how long that would take me. I felt a real sense of relief. All these thoughts went through my mind with the speed of light... I nodded to answer his question; he observed me for a few seconds, seemed to be satisfied with what he saw, nodded back, and went on:

'One other problem I faced was the need to forgive myself for several things I had done in the past. I came to the realization that everything I've just said is true for these kinds of memory too. So, *there is nothing wrong with regretting things one has done in the past – but only for 90 seconds.* Then the mind should be cleared and set free as soon as possible!'

He paused again, and the smile came back on his face while he said: 'But enough about me. Let's go back to you. After all that you have learned, what will be your next step?'

'To be honest that is the main question that occupies me these days...,' I said. 'Can you please give me a sense of direction?'

He hesitated... but said then: 'I don't think I should do that... But let me share some of the most important insights I learned in the past decade or so. I think you're ready for it. Right?'

'Please do,' I said.

'Good. The first insight I want to share is about the two ways to live.'

TWO WAYS TO LIVE

I took some sips from my bottle of water. The Man did the same from his and continued: 'Albert Einstein once said: *"There are only two ways to live: one can live as if nothing is a miracle or as if everything is a miracle."* The difference is huge! Living as if nothing is a miracle is a one way ticket to the 'rat race.'.. Have you ever heard about a flea circus?' he asked.

'Yes I have,' I replied, 'but please explain what you mean by it.'

He nodded and went on. 'Not that long ago a flea circus was part of almost any fun-fair. The tiny little insects that fleas are, were trained to do all kind of acrobatic performances. You can see it yourself on Youtube.com if you want; just search for the words 'flea circus.' Problem is that fleas are normally able to jump a very long distance, so they could easily jump into the audience and get lost. A pity if all the work by the trainer was wasted, and besides, I guess an incoming flea is not that much appreciated by the average member of the public either! So the first thing a flea circus trainer wants to accomplish is to make sure that a flea is not going to jump that far any longer. And that is quite easy: just place the flea in a not too large jar, put the lid on it and leave him there for a while.

'At first the flea will try to escape by jumping, but of course he whacks his head painfully against the jar. After a while the lid can be removed. The flea will *never* jump any higher than the height of the lid in the 'conditioning jar' since a brain circuit has been made which reminds him that jumping any higher is very, very painful. By the same method elephants, apes, dolphins and orcas are conditioned, just to name a few.'

'What the lid does with a flea, society does with men. Leaders on any level prefer *predictable behavior* of 'their' people. They use statistics to make predictions and use communication, advertising, procedures, systems laws, punishment and rewards to keep everyone in a predictable state. With these kinds of techniques they keep the 'mental lid' active. I don't intend to discount this, since, depending on the intention of the leader, these 'tools' can be quite useful. Useful or not, they are just methods to condition the brain and can reasonably be compared to a flea circus.'

'I see what you mean,' I said. 'I read an article about 'socially programmed hypnosis' that describes the same principle.'

'Sure. I saw it in your notes about our 'miraculous brain.' It's exactly what I mean. So, the first way to live - *as if nothing is a miracle* - leads in my experience directly to the rat race and the flea circus, both of which limit your opportunities in life tremendously. The easiest way to understand why, is by taking a closer look at the other way to live.'

'*To live as if* everything *is a miracle... That is the highway to a great life!* And no doubt Albert Einstein himself lived as if everything is a miracle. The reason this way of living is so effective, can be found in the human brain. The first role of every brain is to keep its owner alive. As a logical consequence it tries to understand everything, since any unexpected event might be a threat. In other words: the brain questions everything that is new or unexpected. Questions trigger creativity. *Creativity is the only way out of an existing reality. Creativity is therefore also the only way out of the rat race... the only way out of depression... the only way out of an unfulfilling life...* Creativity is triggered by questions, and questions become abundant when you see everything as a miracle... Are you getting what I mean?'

I didn't answer right away, since my mind was still digesting these simple, but astonishing, insights. Then I heard myself saying, slowly at first, '*Seeing life's miracles... trying to understand them... asking questions... increased creativity... finding solutions... a more fulfilling life...* I think I've got it. It makes a lot of sense. Now I understand the name of the first chapter in the notebook you gave me: *Scientific Inspiration.* And I understand why you often afterwards used the word 'miraculous' in most of its subchapters.'

'Exactly,' he replied. 'And that brings me directly to another insight I want to share with you, which I've named 'Masters and middlemen.'

MASTERS AND MIDDLEMEN

'Middlemen,' he continued without a pause, 'are exactly what the word says: they stand between you and the solution of a problem. Middlemen want to sell you *their* solution; Masters trigger you, inspire you, to find *yours. Middlemen manipulate... Masters liberate...* A Master's life is *consistent* with his words; a middleman's life is most of the times not consistent with his words at all... I know the difference very well, since, as I have told you before, I was a middleman for a long time myself. Although there are some good middlemen and the help of a middleman is sometimes better than no help at all, the main rule is: *Get rid of the middlemen; find your Masters.* Masters, because you need the best one for each subject in which you want to grow.'

'In our culture,' he continued, 'we don't use the word 'Master' that much, but the word 'Mentor' comes close to it. The noun 'mentor' was originally not an ordinary noun at all, but a name: *Mentor was the older, wiser friend* of Odysseus' son Telemachus and a central character in Homer's famous epic poem the *Odyssey*. A nice detail is that the Greek name 'Telemachus' literally means *'far from the battle.'* So if we go back to the roots, a mentor is 'an older, wiser friend whose influence keeps the younger one far from the battle...' In that meaning almost anyone would love to have a mentor. The relatively recent growth in the number of coaches and mentors all over the globe is, as I see it, an illustration of the need for Masters or Mentor'Middlemen,' he said, while I saw a look of mild distaste on his face, 'are frequently found in organized religions. Many priests and pastors want you to believe that they have a better knowledge of God... a more direct relation with God... and that they know better how to serve Him... The only things most middlemen want you to do are to obey and to donate substantially. But don't get me wrong: in each religion there are real Masters as well, those who really want you to grow and who stimulate you to do so. I don't know, and don't have to know, if you go to a church, but *always be sure you understand the difference between a master and a middleman*, not only in church by the way. Whenever you hesitate in deciding if someone is a master or a middleman, listen to your intuition, the voice of your subconscious mind. Your intuition knows the difference between a Master and a middleman within the first 30 seconds after meeting the individual, or at least by the end of the first meeting. How? Because while your Left Brain listens to what is said, your Right Brain looks continuously for inconsistencies between the words of any speaker and his body language and tone of voice. All signals are compared at a subconscious level and the outcome will be presented to you through your intuition. *'Can't intuition be wrong?'* you might ask. The answer is, 'Yes, but seldom.' A far larger problem is that too many people are not even able to hear the voice of their intuition...'

'What do you mean?' I asked.

'Well... *Intuition doesn't shout, it whispers*. When you are too stressed, too busy, too prejudiced for whatever reason, you will just miss the intuition's signals. It's as simple as that. Turning off the 'sound level' of your intuition is one of the life threatening dangers of stress. Stress sets the 'sound level' of almost anything in daily life to that of a modern dance club: so loud that people cannot even understand each other and they literarily will become deaf. *Many, many people have either never developed their intuition, or else have become deaf to its voice...* Both are life threatening!'

The Man looked at me, giving me the opportunity to put a question, but I didn't care to interrupt him. After a few seconds he resumed talking. 'Masters and middlemen are found in many other fields of life as well. The family doctor, for example, who during a visit may already be writing a prescription, almost before you can finish your very first sentence, so to speak. Such behavior makes it likely that he is the typical middleman, not a Master, despite his education, credentials or reputation. But please understand me: there are, of course, plenty of real Masters in the medical profession as well.'

'In Buddhism' he went on, 'there's a proverb that says: *'If you find the Buddha, kill him!'* It took me a very long time to understand the meaning. Buddha was a Master, no doubt at all about that. So why kill him? Once we skip the literal meaning, the proverb starts to make sense, since even a great Master can be dangerous for personal growth: in the situation where a student merely quotes the Master's words, and only copies, let's suppose, outward ritual behavior, without really developing his own force, he uses the Master more like a middleman. In that case, it's better to get rid of the Master... better to 'kill the Buddha.' You got me?'

And again I nodded, allowing the Man to continue. 'Just one more thing on this subject. I am glad you liked your Personal Scan, as I learned from your notes on it. The Personal Scan can be a great tool for any good coach or mentor; I use these two words as synonyms. The coach can help his student to deeply understand his scan and the theory behind it. He can explain the many psychological meanings in the various graphs and the Personality Icon. He can help to understand the meaning of the so called 'blind spot' and to avoid its pitfalls. He can help his student to better understand others by using the

Personality Icons, and to substantially improve both personal as well as professional relations in teams and organizations. He can also help find out what professions would be ideally suited, given a Personality Type. Just to mention a few… A good Personality Coach should be experienced as a mentor, an older and wiser friend. The word 'older' in this context should be understood as 'more experienced.'

'*Everyone needs one or more good, wise friends,*' he went on, 'Anyone needs a mentor. At least one. You can live without this for a while, but not too long. That mentor can be your partner in life. It can be just a friend. It can be a professional coach or mentor. But unquestionably you do need one, simply because only a real friend is able to give you honest feedback about anything in your life in a way you will trust and accept… *No-one can see his own face without a mirror!* It is not important at all how often friends meet, nor how far they live apart, and their ages play no role either. The only thing that counts is *the quality of their relationship as they both experience it.* A mentor should be not just a friend, but a 'wiser friend' as the Odyssey showed its audience about 2800 years ago. Any questions?'

'At least one…,' I said hesitating, 'We have had such intimate conversations and I don't even know your name. I didn't want to ask your name till now, but I would love to be able to reach you in case I need it.' Seeing the frown on his face, I added 'I will not contact you if it is not really needed of course.'

He was silent for a moment and then said with a soft voice: 'You are actually asking two things: my name and my address. Although I don't have objections to sharing those with you, I am always reluctant to do so, since the very fact that you *can* reach me changes your growth process. That can become better, or it can become worse. So… what about this?' and he handed me a kind of business card; there was no name on it, only a kind of generic email address that I cannot write here, of course, for privacy reasons. He said: 'This is how you can reach me. It's not my name, but it is a contact. Don't be disappointed when I don't reply to some emails, or only after quite a long time. And about a name… How do you refer to me in your mind at the moment?'

'I call you 'Mentor,' I replied, 'as in the Odyssey.'

'I like that!' he said, 'Why would we change it?' And in my turn I liked it too.

He took some sips from his bottle of water and stared silently over the sea for some time, just like me. In the few weeks following this meeting I did some research into mentors and coaches. I found two movie characters that are really great coaches in exactly the way the Man characterized them that day in Ruckle Park. One was Mr Keating, the English teacher in *Dead Poets Society* and the other was Lionel Logue, the voice coach of King George VI in the movie *The King's Speech* (based on a true story). I had no desire to find a mentor myself, since I had already found one and he was sitting next to me on a bench in Ruckle Park. It was his insight about Masters and middlemen that made me stop calling him 'the Man': I just named him 'Mentor,' as in the Odyssey. I'd never read the Odyssey completely, but a sufficiently large part to know, that it's a story about a long journey back home. That was exactly the feeling I got listening to Mentor: I was finally on my journey back home…

Luckily enough the meeting in Ruckle Park was not over yet. After a few minutes Mentor turned his attention to me again and said, 'There are some more insights I want to share with you. Three basic principles of life. Are you ready?'

'Sure. Please go on!' I replied.

THE LAW OF RADIANCE

'The first principle is what I call 'The Law of Radiance.' Everything in the universe has a measurable radiance, we humans as well. It is composed of electromagnetic waves that radiate from our body as well as from our body language, our voice, our tone of voice, and our smell too. In the same way as a shock has an instant impact on all cells of our body, all of our thoughts, feelings and emotions have a discernible impact on our radiance. So never forget: your *state of mind* is *mirrored* in your *radiance* and will be felt by everyone, profoundly! The salesperson, for example, who visits a customer he really hates, is very unlikely to sell anything; simply because the customer will sense the salesperson's strong dislike. When I was young, my parents often warned me that they knew when I told lies, since 'it was written on my forehead.' Well, that is actually quite true; not literally, but telling a lie is revealed in your radiance like everything else. There is a kind of a mental lie-detector embedded in our subconscious.'

Mentor continued without interruption: 'We all like to be in the presence of a person with a strong radiance. We admire them, sometimes even without knowing it. Actually this admiration is another aspect of Brain Efficiency: the brain knows that we can learn from those people and want therefore to be in their presence and experience their radiance. Look at the behavior of fans of any famous person: they want to be as close as possible to their hero, without exactly knowing why. Fans feel each other's passion as well, which multiplies the energy in that field of radiance.'

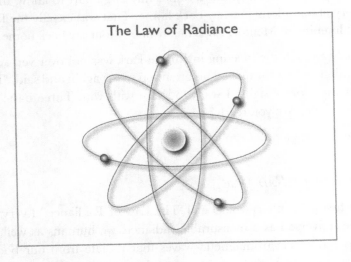

The Law of Radiance

'The Law of Radiance simply says'

Your life will be as great as your Radiance.

'So you might ask: "How can I boost my Radiance?" Well… it all starts with '*Know Thyself*.' No one can build a strong radiance without Self Knowledge. It is the start of a very interesting series of qualities:

- *Self Knowledge* ('know thyself') builds Self Confidence
- *Self Confidence* builds Self Esteem
- *Self Esteem* builds strong Radiance
- *Strong Radiance* creates Blessing Relationships
- *Blessing Relationships* give useful Feedback
- *Feedback* increases Self Knowledge

And a spiral of Personal Growth is created. Makes sense, doesn't it?'

'No doubt it does.' And I confessed, 'To be honest it was *your* radiance that I instantly recognized when I saw you the very first time in Stanley Park'

'Me as well!' he said. And I was silent for a while, not sure how to place this remark. Mentor did not wait for me and said:

'As you have found out in the meantime, understanding your personality is essential to gain sufficient Self Knowledge. *Understanding your Personality is the 'root of your radiance,'* so to speak. That explains why a whole chapter of the notebook—Personality Matters—was dedicated to this subject. Personality matters, of course; it matters a lot in relationships as well, since any relationship is the interaction of at least two Personalities. In a direct relationship (one person relating to one other, sometimes noted as 1:1, or one-to-one) there are 4 options: both persons have, or neither has, sufficient Self Knowledge, or the one has and the other hasn't. Can you imagine what a difference can be seen in the interaction between people in each of these four options? The level of Self Knowledge of each person makes all the difference in the world for the quality of any relationship! Strangely enough, our society doesn't pay much attention to these fundamental principles, but I hope that this will change now we are in a far more creative phase of the global society.'

'Far more creative?!' I said at once, 'I thought we were in an economic crises.'

He smiled. 'No, we are not. That's wishful thinking.' Which confused me even more, but luckily Mentor explained: 'Any economic crisis will be over after a few years. Not this one. *We are not in an* economic *crisis: we are in the midst of a* fundamental *change that will change society for ever… completely!* Within a few decades history will be teaching that we live in a period of change at least as big as the Renaissance and the Industrial Revolution! The *tsunami of change* flooding our great little planet is destroying a lot of the old certainties… a lot of the things we took for granted. People will have to change old habits, which is a creative process. So, no doubt, we are in a very creative phase all over the globe. But creativity is not just about fun: pain and hard work are indispensable parts of it as well, as every mother can tell you at the birth of her first child. Are you clear on what I mean?'

'It sounds pretty logical,' I said, 'but I should give that some more thought and let it have time to digest…'

'As you should do with all my words,' he joked. But for me this was no joke at all. I began to understand that Mentor had a completely different view from mine on just about anything. More and more I got the feeling that, thanks to his influence in my life, I was breaking through a kind of mental ceiling and was suddenly able to discover whole new worlds… Which reminded me of the lid on the jar with the fleas, and that made me laugh. Apparently, Mentor interpreted that as a signal to go on:

'A couple more things on this Law of Radiance. First and foremost this: it would be hard to find better ways to boost your radiance than by *meditation*, physical *exercise* and a healthy *diet*… I sometimes call them together the Trinity or *the Holy Grail of Wellbeing*. We can easily understand the health benefits of exercise and diet, but too many people are still not familiar with those of meditation. The tremendous benefit of meditation is confirmed by scientists and medical doctors all over the globe. Dr Deepak Chopra, for example, called meditation 'the single most important thing I learned in life.' Meditation not only calms the mind and relieves stress, it opens the mind also for a deeper understanding of life at all levels. Meditation aligns your brain waves and boosts your radiance. These results are not obtained only after years of meditation: the benefits start immediately and become substantial within a few weeks. Are you a meditator?'

'No, I'm not,' I replied, 'Not yet. The only thing I know about meditation is that there are many forms and some of them are connected to religions or even sects. Can you recommend a good form of meditation?'

'No, since I don't like to give advice any longer, as you know. But,' he smiled, 'I can tell you which form I use: it is called Primordial Sound Meditation. Just google these words and you'll find teachers all over the world. And yes, there are forms of meditation that are connected to churches and sects, but meditation itself is definitely not linked to any particular such group: *meditation is just a technique one can learn. And it should be taught in that way.* But as you know, while churches and sects may use the alphabet to write all kinds of holy books, that doesn't disqualify the alphabet. In much the same way, the use of meditation in religious organizations doesn't disqualify meditation. But there's no doubt we should always be careful when choosing a meditation technique or a teacher. One more thing on this subject: advanced meditators learn to use *sutras*, as they are called. A *sutra* consists of special words or sounds that are mentally connected to special parts of the body. I was—and still am—touched especially by the four Heart Sutras. Those are:'

'Peace   Harmony   Laughter   Love'

'Four inner qualities that are so important... Simply sitting with your eyes closed and silently repeating these four words, changes your brain in the right direction. When anyone deeply feels these qualities in his or her heart, the radiance will be so strong... so very strong. By the way, if you want an example of the impact of the Law of Radiance: see the movie 'Gandhi.' Even the trailer of this move, and you can see it on Youtube, will instantly show what I mean by the Law of Radiance.'

'Over the last decade I have developed the habit of asking myself a simple question for nearly every conscious choice I make: 'Would doing that increase or decrease my radiance?' A variant that I use when I become angry and feel like getting into a verbal fight, is: 'Can I say what I want to say without losing my radiance? Can I say what I want to say with an honest smile?' The answer to this kind of inner question is most times given by our subconscious mind; the conscious mind often tries to override that answer, but it's better to listen to the voice of our subconscious. These simple questions have saved me a lot of negative energy... But let's move on; we've been here for quite some time and there is more I'd like to share with you. That is to say, if you still have some time available and want me to go on.'

I answered, 'Oh yes, please do. I'm not in a hurry at all. I hope I'm not taking up too much of your time?'

'Young man, no one can take any of my time... nor yours either. Time is the one commodity that is evenly distributed among all of us for as long as we live: everyone gets a fresh slice of 24 hours every day. *No-one but myself masters my time. Time cannot be spent. Time cannot be wasted. Time can only be used and enjoyed, or not...* But,' he said in a friendly way, 'I know what you meant. So let it be time for the next of my three laws: the 'Law of Abundance.'

THE LAW OF ABUNDANCE

'Life is abundant, wonderfully abundant,' Mentor said with a broad movement of his arm gesturing to everything around our little bench in Ruckle Park. 'A universe packed with stars, planets and light... millions of species of plants, trees and animals... trillions of cells in our body... whole clouds of pollen in spring... a millions of sperms when only one is needed... abundance everywhere! Have you ever thought about why life is so abundant?'

'Actually no,' I replied, and thought for a while, 'but now you've made me think about it... I guess that, from those last examples, abundance creates greater opportunity to survive than scarcity, doesn't it?'

'Exactly!' Mentor exclaimed with energy, as if he'd just started our conversation, 'Exactly! Since there is no certainty in life, it needs to create abundant possibilities for survival. Since all of us are a part of nature as well, the same is true for us: *since we can't create certainty, we had best create abundant opportunities for what we want.* Abundant in quantity and abundant in quality. If we want a job, it's better to write

1000 letters than 10. If we want to get 25 people enrolled in a course, we should reach out to several thousands. And so on. Moreover, we'd make sure that the quality of those letters is high: quality in 'look and feel,' in use of language, in attractiveness of content and in the ways the receivers of the letters can respond. Be aware that *'quality' is always defined by the receiver*: it's not *my* opinion which defines the quality of my communications, but what is experienced by 'the other.' And the best way to find out is: *ask them... get feedback!*'

'Quantity and quality have an inverse relation in the Law of Abundance: *the better the quality of the input, the less quantity of input is needed to make a particular outcome likely...* which means: to accomplish a certain goal. Most people are raised with the idea that hard work is good... Working hard is a positive habit. Isn't it? Do you see the birds working hard to get their food? I don't think so... But no doubt they are effective; they work well (which is about quality) but not hard (which is about quantity). Don't get me wrong: naturally I don't preach laziness. *Yet it's quite clear that simply working hard is no longer enough to create abundance.* Quality and creativity have become much more important than before; *they* are today's key to abundance.'

Mentor was silent for a moment and then added, 'It is important to really understand the essence of the Law of Abundance, since there is a lot of misunderstanding, especially in so-called 'success programs' that often promise to reveal special secrets via books, audios, videos, courses, or conferences. Most of that literature wants you to believe that you can *have* everything you really want: money, perfect health, abundant sex, a long life... you name it. If you don't get what you want, you 'didn't really try'... or you didn't really believe in it... that is to say, it's what these 'success programs' want you to believe. But it's nonsense... *absolutely nonsense.*Mentor sighed deeply. 'What those authors write would seem to mean that one of my neighbors, who recently died from cancer, did not try hard enough to recover or did not really believe in her opportunity to survive... It would mean that those three soldiers who died yesterday in Afghanistan didn't try hard enough to stay alive... What an awful and disrespectful view of life that would be! The major mistake the authors of these books make is, that they assume it's possible to create anything *with certainty,* just so long as the right insights are gained and the right methods are used. Once again: that's absolutely nonsensical. *Since the discovery of Quantum Mechanics we know that even in the physical world, which obeys all of the natural laws, nothing can be created or predicted with complete certainty.* If that is the case in nature itself, would we human beings be able to create whatever we want?? No go! But on the other hand, one should not think the opposite: that whatever we do, it makes no sense, since all is pre-destined. *What we can do—always and in every circumstance—is make it very likely that what will happen is what we want to happen.* That's the *vision* behind the Law of Abundance.'

'However, don't get me wrong: this does not mean that every book about success is no good. My good friend Deepak Chopra wrote a global best seller entitled *The Seven Spiritual Laws of Success,* for example, and I'd say it's a must-read for everyone. Did you ever read it?'

'No, I didn't,' I replied.

'You should, I truly think. It would be hard to get deeper insights for just a couple of bucks. Deepak's 'great little book' is one of the very few books on success that is based on well-understood principles of the universe. Not many people know that Deepak Chopra's original title for that book was *The Seven Laws of Life,* but it was changed by his publisher, for good reasons by the way. Any questions so far?'

'Only one,' I said. 'How do we apply the Law of Abundance? How do we make it very likely that we create the life we want?'

'Thank you for asking, since that brings us directly to the *action* in the Law of Abundance. Please tell me: what is absolutely needed to create anything new?'

I pondered for a minute and replied: 'An *idea?*'

'That's right!' said Mentor. 'So let's take a practical example: you get the idea to make changes in your garden. Once you have that idea, what's the next step?'

It didn't take me long to answer that one: 'A *plan* and a budget, I assume?'

'You hit the nail on the head again!' Mentor said enthusiastically, 'Actually a budget is just a part of the plan, like any permits that are required, or licenses and any of the whole orchestra of formalities that seem to be necessary these days to do anything. It's hard even to bake a cake without a permit,' he joked. 'So, once your plan is finished: what's next?'

'Nike.,' I responded.

He was confused for a moment: 'What do you mean?'

'Just *do* it!'

His laugh was spontaneous, as soon as he recognized the catchphrase. He said: 'You got me! But you are exactly right: the third step in human creation, since that is what we are talking about, is just doing it: after planning the work, it's time to work the plan... You will understand that sYstematic types pay a lot attention to step 2, the planning, while that same phase will normally get the minimal attention by the more iMprovising types. But in both types the planning is followed by 'doing,' unless, of course, the planning phase leads to the conclusion that it would be better not to go on at all.' So what comes after the work is done... after the plan has been executed?'

That was a tougher question. A finished plan is a finished plan... is there anything after it? 'I don't really know...,' I said with some hesitation.

'No problem.' Mentor said, 'Let me answer this question myself. After doing, one gets *a result*. Results trigger three consequent actions:'

- '*Celebration*: getting a result is normally a reason to celebrate. Celebrations are no luxury, in contrary: a celebration expresses that the accomplished results could not be created with certainty, but are a reason to be graceful. *Gracefulness is an attitude that recognizes the miracle.*'

- '*Maintenance*: once your garden is finished, it should better be maintained well. Maintenance should better be part of the original plan. And executed conform plan. Otherwise even the best result can over time become a disaster.'

- '*Feedback*: feedback is raising the question '*Is the result conform the original idea and plan?*' The answer is not alway 'yes' of course... There is not always a reason to celebrate the results of even the best plan.

When there is no reason to celebrate, there is often an opportunity to learn.
I termed these three steps together 'align'; why will become clear when we talk about the last Law.'

'Makes sense?' he asked.

You bet!' I said. Mentor took his wallet and gave me a kind of a business card that looked like the next picture.

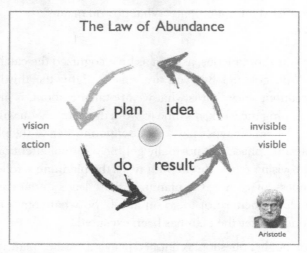

Then he explained: 'So now we have four elements: idea—plan—do—result. These 4 steps were originally formulated by Aristotle about 2400 years ago; he termed them 'The Four Causes.' Each step causes the next one. Only the Gods, wrote Aristotle, can create results directly from an idea; we humans can only create by following all four steps. I find it handy to present Aristotle's Four Causes in two pairs of two 'elements of creation,' like you see on the card. The first two elements (getting ideas and making plans) are mainly done in the mind and therefore mostly 'invisible'; together I call them 'Vision.' The other two (the actual 'doing' and the 'results'—are quite visible; together I call them 'Action.'

Mentor did the summarizing:

'Creating Abundance is blending Vision and Action.
Vision without Action is only dreaming.
Action without Vision is just a waste of time.
Only the synergy of Vision and Action can create Abundance.'

'This 'Vision and Action' model is as simple as it is powerful. Agreed?'

I nodded and he went on: 'There is one more thing to say about this law: *abundance always starts by giving.* You can't harvest without sowing. If you want to harvest rye, you better not sow wheat. If you want to become wealthy, sow ideas, create plans and take actions that are worthwhile in society. If you want to harvest health, you need to live healthy. If you want to harvest happiness, you'd better sow happiness. If you want to harvest friendliness, you have to be friendly. If you want to harvest trust, you have to be reliable, a person to trust. Once more: you don't have to work *hard*, you just have to work *well.*'

'Whatever you want to get, give it!'

'When everyone does this, all of society will be abundant. The members of that society, which can be as small as a family or as big as the planet, will together generate all ideas needed, give their talents to make good plans, collaborate to realize them and celebrate and share the results. That's what, in my opinion, John Lennon meant when he wrote his most famous song 'Imagine'…'

Mentor continued almost without interruption, 'Unfortunately we lost sight of the Law of Abundance the moment we introduced 'money' as a means to facilitate sharing. Instead of a means of exchange, *having* money became a goal in itself. There is nothing wrong with the desire to earn money. But don't do *anything* for the sake of money; do what you do only because you want to do it, want to give, want to share… And then gracefully accept what you are given in exchange. That's the only way to keep the flow of Abundance going. Don't waste your time on people who don't want to give back, since they frustrate the flow of Abundance, in your life as in theirs. And don't 'only work,' but find your 'element,' and do what is your passion, give in areas you are good in, and receive gracefully what you get in return. When what you receive is not really enough, don't look for the solution in quantity, but in quality. In other words: don't work harder, but work better. Change the way you work, change the work you do, or change the people you work for or work with. Don't forget to use your Personal Scan as a point of reference for your decisions. So, let's get on to the last principle: the Law of Alignment.'

THE LAW OF ALIGNMENT

'The last principle I term 'The Law of Alignment.' When we were young all of us liked to play with magnets. You know why? Playing with some iron filings and a magnet is the very first conscious experience of the Law of Alignment. It's magical. We see that an invisible force is not only connecting all particles of the iron filings in a mysterious way, but literally arranging them in certain patterns.

'And those are exactly the two dimensions of the Law of Alignment: it *connects and coordinates towards a certain point or a certain purpose*. Everything in the universe is aligned: the sub-atomic particles in an atom, the atoms in a molecule, the molecules in a DNA string, the DNA in all cells, the cells in an organ, the organs in a living body, all creatures on a planet, all planets in this solar system, the solar systems in a galaxy, the galaxies in the universe... it's all aligned. Every part is this huge 'magical orchestra' just 'does its own thing' while at the same time it contributes to the whole. That's alignment. Got it?'

And he continued without waiting for my answer, 'If you want to see another magical visualization of the Law of Alignment, google the word '*cymatics*.' It will lead you to a website where you will read, see and hear how sound and form are aligned in a beautiful, astonishing way.'

'Alignment is actually composed of several sub-processes, which can easily be understood by looking at living organisms:'

- '*Unity*: all living creatures are either one cell or grew from one cell. The 'imprint' of that one cell is present in the DNA of any other cell.'

- '*Specialization*: the first cell divides and multiplies. In the beginning the resulting cells are exact copies of 'cell one' and are called 'stem cells.' Later on they specialize and form organs, networks of cells with special tasks, which can form networks of networks as well.'

- '*Collaboration*: cells not only collaborate within their specific organ, but in their turn the organs collaborate within the body.'

- '*Feedback*: to keep our body temperature at about 98° Fahrenheit or 37° Celsius, for example, some organs have to measure that temperature and send the information to the brain; the brain, then, has to decide what actions have to be taken based on the received information and it has to send instructions for these actions to other organs. That process is continuously repeated, and is called a 'feedback loop.' Feedback processes are in most organisms handled by the nervous system.'

- '*Communication*: any good collaboration requires a two-way communication, as already illustrated talking about feedback.'
- '*Learning*: learning is in essence nothing more than a form of brain efficiency: experiences are stored for future use…'

'All these processes are natural principles that, together, keep the universe aligned at all levels, all the time. Alignment is not only essential in living organisms, but in all aspects of the universe.'

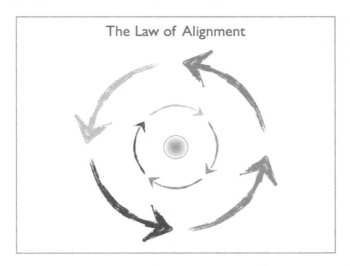

The Law of Alignment

'When alignment is disturbed,' Mentor went on, full speed, 'the organism is sick. *Being healthy is being fully aligned at all levels*; everything works fine on all levels. *Healing is returning to full alignment at all levels*. These are extremely important insights! Do you understand them?'

'I think I do,' I replied, speaking slowly. It would still take me a while to digest this new way of understanding health and healing. 'Is there a special reason why you repeated the words 'at all levels' several times?'

'You bet! A simple reason: I repeated these words to emphasize their importance. You know, when one of your organs is sick, the whole you is sick. When your mind is depressed or stressed, your whole body is depressed and stressed as well. When your body is overweight, another example, your mind is too heavy as well: your senses are spoiled, your thinking is not that alert, you are not as fast and flexible as you used to be, your feelings become sentimental and your intuition is weak. As a result you might even put on unwanted weight. Do you recognize anything here?'

'I most certainly do.' I replied promptly, 'And it makes a lot of sense, although I have never seen this obvious coherence between all aspects of life so clearly before.'

'You are not alone in that, my friend. Generation after generation go to school for more than 15 years on average, and learn a lot from books, but almost nothing about ourselves. This is such a pity, for if we don't learn what we need to learn in our early years, we have to learn it later in life. Life will remind us, through its very imaginative way of creating endless series of problems — which will sooner or later get us thinking.'

'Once you clearly see the Law of Alignment, you start to understand why no one can keep to a diet while still being unhappy. Or why tranquilizers can slow down the nerves but don't solve the underlying problem. If you really want to come out of your depression forever, you have to obey the Law of Alignment and make major changes in all unaligned aspects of your life. *You have to deepen your soul, clear your mind, strengthen your body, boost your radiance, renew your relationships, improve your home, redefine your work, grow your wealth and take care of your environment… all in a quite short span of time.* You have to boost the alignment in all aspects of life more or less simultaneously.'

He paused for a while, observing me, and continued. 'That seems like a mission impossible, but it isn't… it isn't at all! What is impossible is to bring about lasting improvements in just one or two aspects of your life, *while neglecting the others*; that's against the Law of Alignment and it's a lost race before it starts. Boosting alignment in all aspects of life is not that difficult at all: once you really understand the absolute necessity to align all aspects of your life, take a firm decision to do so, and just start! The results will be so good, so very very encouraging that you never ever want to go back to your old habits... Moreover, *through 'full alignment'—that is, aligning your soul, your mind, your body and everything and everyone around you—you create the optimal circumstances for living a great life*... Without alignment, the struggle will go on... forever!'

He stopped and looked at me, obviously curious about my reaction. It didn't take me too long to say, with a smile, 'At least you sound quite convincing.' With a big smile he replied: 'Of course! But it's getting late and I am getting a bit chilled. Unless you have pressing questions, I suggest we wind up our meeting.'

'I actually do have one simple question,' I replied. 'What are the pitfalls I should know about before going any further in this adventure?'

He laughed loudly. 'How many weeks do you have for the answer? Life is full of pitfalls! We need them to grow...'

Everyone is entitled to solve his own problems.

So, maybe better I don't warn you at all. Or just a few, in telegram style... enough to prompt you to think for yourself.'

LIFE'S PITFALLS

Here is what Mentor said about the pitfalls in life:

- 'Pitfall 1: *Positive thinking.* It sounds so good, but it isn't. When eating beef, it might be good for *you*, but it's not for the *cow*. What is positive for you can be bad for someone else. Thinking in terms of good and bad, positive and negative, has a long history, including in Christianity, which takes its followers back to the time Eve ate that apple: the apple from the *'tree of knowledge of good and evil'* as we can read in the Old Testament. You might know that the words 'of good and evil' were originally not in the source writings at all, but were added in the 4th century by the founding fathers of the Church. In the original documents (written in Aramaic, the original language of the initial books of the Bibles' Old Testament) is only written that Eve ate from '*the tree of knowledge*'. Full stop. The Aramaic word for 'knowledge' also meant 'consciousness.' So Eve ate from '*the tree of consciousness*,' a process all of us went through in our very first years. We start life, for example, without any idea of time, yesterday, tomorrow and death, but at a certain moment we become conscious about these concept; from that moment on we can never return to 'not being conscious'… we can never return to that uncomplicated, peaceful state, that 'Garden of Eden'. Life is not about good and bad, positive and negative; life is about conscious living! Please contemplate this for the sake of your own future. So…, positive thinking is a pitfall, just as negative thinking is; it's an infantile form of thinking, often used in 'success books' to sway people. We should leave the word positive out, and also the word negative, and just be conscious of what is and what happens…'

'Mmm…' Mentor went on, 'that was not really in telegram style, was it? Let me try to be shorter.'

- 'Pitfall 2: *Expectations*. I often forget that it is *me* who raises the expectation, thereby sowing the seed of disappointment. Others might trigger my expectations, but no one else but me raises the bar! No-one can be disappointed without having expectation. So we should be careful in creating expectations about others. We should be even more careful in triggering expectation in others about ourselves. 'Under-promise and over-deliver' is still a great recipe!'

- 'Pitfall 3: *Trust*. The third pitfall is trust, or we might call it reliability. Although we cannot live without it, we should realize that trust is just a kind of expectation. So exactly the same mechanics apply to trust as are written above about expectations. There is that great Sufi saying: '*Trust in Allah, but don't forget to tie your camel*'. Which means: you can trust people and at the same time reduce your risks. In business, for example, shaking hands is a great way to confirm an agreement and to express the mutual trust; but in today's society it better can be followed by a signed agreement, also among friends! Key is to be reliable yourself. Always. And in the event that you fall short: own up, pay for the damage, and learn from the whole experience.'

- 'Pitfall 4: *Must*. The fourth pitfall is the family of *'musts.'* We tend to think that we have too many obligations in life, too many musts. But who created my musts? No one else but me! Maybe we should just say 'No' more often. Moreover, most 'musts' are not musts at all. Years ago I gave a lecture and at the end a woman made a statement: *"You give the impression that we have a lot of freedom to create our own life, but I don't think that's realistic. In reality our freedom is very limited by a lot of things we really have to do. Life is in reality often a long list of 'musts.'* I asked her to give an example and she said: *'I have two young daughters that take, next to my job, almost every minute of my time. So, almost no freedom for me.'* I thanked her for the clear example and I asked her: *"Do you know people in more or less the same situation, who simply walk away from their children and from all those musts?"* She replied instantly: *"Of course I do, but that's not what I want!"* I looked direct in her eyes for a few seconds and said slowly: *"Can you please repeat what you just said?."* She looked amazed, but started: *"I said: of course I do, but that's not what I ..."* and before she spoke the last word her eyes went wide open as if in shock, and after a few seconds big tears appeared: she had suddenly understood that she had been free all the time, but had just labeled her choices in life as a 'must', things she actually had chosen voluntarily. *Don't label things as a must, otherwise they will soon become too heavy.* Stop the heavy-duty 'musts' as soon as possible and label all other things as something you do because you *want* them to do.'

- 'Pitfall 5: *Poisoning Relationships,* which can be found in many parts of life, but especially in marriage and in business. A relationship is a blessing, neutral, or is toxic. *In a blessing-type relationship both parties flourish and grow. In a poisoning relationship one party is destroying the mental energy of the other, or even worse: they are destroying each other.* Neutral relationships, in which parties don't bless but do not damage each other, are actually rare in private life, although many relationships sometimes go through a neutral phase. *Only blessing relationships are sustainable.* Blessing relationships are not blessing all the time and can face severe difficulties as well, but these can be overcome since the basis of the relation is blessing. Then we can also call them blessed. Both poisoning as well as neutral relationships are a waste of time and energy, and dangerous for health because of the stress they bring; such relationships need to be transformed into blessing ones, *or else they should end.* 'If you can't change the people, change the people.' Pitfall 6: *Greed.* This is obvious as one of the biggest pitfalls in life: greed. Greed stops the abundance of the universe in its tracks. Greedy people will always stay *emotionally poor,* however much money they may possess. So don't go for money: go for true wealth. Earning a decent amount of money is not bad, and having a substantial amount of money is not bad either. On the contrary, having good 'buffers,' including financially, can well be one of your objectives. But never let it make you greedy.'

Mentor paused for a moment, obviously thinking how to continue. Then he said: 'And finally, the last pitfall for the moment... *the pitfall of all pitfalls:*

Living without fully enjoying your life
and accepting that as normal...

There are plenty more pitfalls, but this is a good series to start with. That's quite enough to work on, isn't it?'

'And now I really have to go!' he said unexpectedly. 'Good bye, young man...,' Mentor spoke with affection. 'I know you will do well... *very* well! I am grateful for the opportunity you've given me to share some of my lessons in life.'

'I thank you... from the bottom of my heart!' I spoke with deep emotion. 'There are no words that really can express what I feel at this moment... nor to convey my gratitude!'

He looked at me and said, with another of his warm smiles, 'In that case, *just express your gratitude in the way you live.*'

We embraced and shook hands. Then he turned around and walked out of my life. I've never seen him again to this day... But what he touched in me is with me all the time.

'There are two ways to live:

you can live as if nothing is a miracle;

you can live as if everything is a miracle.'

Albert Einstein

Defining My Vision

The next day, back in Vancouver, I bought two good notebooks. On one I wrote 'Vision' and on the other 'Action.' I am still making notes in both, almost daily; that's to say, in additional notebooks, because I soon filled the original ones

It took me a while to find my way in writing... Making notes about subjects you get from someone else is quite different from writing about your own vision in life and about the actual progress you make. But I guarantee it's worthwhile!!!

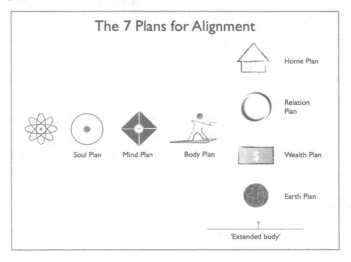

What took some time, too, was developing a Vision about my future. It's weird: after so many years of more or less following and quoting what others had said, it is surprisingly hard to make your own vision on life clear. But I kept working on it, and after a while I found a format that helped me a lot; it is composed of *Seven Aligned Plans* as you see above.

The schema starts with a symbolic atom; I don't use this symbol any further in my plans; it's just to remind me about the importance of my radiance in all plans. Then the Soul, Mind and Body Plan, to be followed by plans for my 'extended bodies': my relations, my home, my wealth and my environment, the part of Planet Earth I am allowed to use. I refer to the combined plan as 'My Vision Statement.'

Of course it makes no sense to publish the literal content of my personal *Vision Statement*, since that is just private. It makes no sense for you, my dear reader, either, since the key for *you* lies not in *my* vision on life, but in *yours*. I hope for you, that you might be inspired to start writing yours as soon as possible. It only needs a firm decision… *now*! When you do, write that decision down, in your own words… and you have already started. No doubt you will experience, as I did, that a firm decision like that gives you instantly a good mental energy.

And then… just go on. Never give up, and only change direction, if needed. Of course, change texts whenever needed, since your Vision Statement is *a living document* that grows as you grow. Normally there are quite a few changes in text in the beginning, but later on the text stabilizes… since *you* get more stable!

Below I will share some of my general notes for each of these seven plans. No personal information, just general notes. Whenever I leave personal notes out, I will indicate that by writing '_____'. A nice challenge for you would be to think about what you would write on these lines, or if you would leave it out completely and why… Please realize: these plans are not meant as a kind of a 'template,' only as inspiration.

I hope that my notes help you on your trip back home…

Back home to your real Self…

Not the Self that others want you to be…

but the Self only you know you are…

1. MY SOUL PLAN

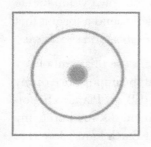

Vision

- While my mind, body and environment change all the time, the real Me doesn't change and doesn't grow older at all. That real Me is what I call my Soul…

- My Soul is a spark of the Universe. I don't know exactly how the Universe and I relate, but I know and feel that we do. I want to experience that connectedness every day of my life…

- I am not afraid of death. I had no problem before I was born and no doubt I will not have a problem after death…

- I am not afraid to live. Life is as it is… with its ups and its downs, its pleasures and its pains. Life is a miracle and living an art…

- I want to fill my life with peace, harmony, laughter and love…

- Like everyone, I have immensely more talents than I will be able to develop during my lifetime. So I can either develop several of my talents, but not develop them that far, or I can decide to focus and deeply develop one or two of my Core Talents. Core Talents are those talents that let me forget time while I am using them, and that fill me with enthusiasm and energy…

Action Plans

- My core talents are: _____
- The talents I will develop are: _____
- I will not waste my talents, nor my time.
- Nature is the temple of life. I will go out in nature, often, or as much as I can, at least _____
- Arts help to open the soul for the miracle and the unexpected. The arts I enjoy the most are: _____
- I will make time for experiencing art, at least _____
- I will perform the following art(s) myself: _____
- I want music, an art as well of course, to become an important part of my life. The music I really like is _____
- I will make time for experiencing music, at least _____
- The instrument(s) I will play is (are): _____
- I will not be my own judge in art music or anything else. I don't have to be super-good at anything to enjoy it.
- I will not only do what I am used to, but will be open for new experiences and the unexpected as well. I will not plan any action on this

point, since that kills the surprise. But I definitely want to be open to the new.

- I am open for change as well, but that's not a goal in itself.
- I will meditate, on a regular basis, since is connects my Soul with the Universe and aligns all energy in me and around me. The form of meditation I will use is _____
- I will meditate, at least _____

2. MY MIND PLAN

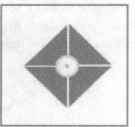

Vision

- My Mind is the captain of my ship of life. It is the beginning, middle and end of anything that happens to me and by me...
- I am the master of my conscious Mind, me and no one else...
- My subconscious will help me to better align all aspects of life. I will make sure that I can hear its voice: my intuition...

- I realize that everyone and everything around me shapes a substantial part of my brain, literally. I will be careful who and what I give access to my Mind...
- I realize that everyone needs at least one Mentor, a more experienced, wiser friend...
- I want to be or become a mentor myself as well...
- I realize that I cannot change my history, but also that I *can* change how I think and feel about anything that happened and will happen. I will not be a prisoner of my own thoughts and will digest and let go what I should, to set myself free...
- I will continue to study my Personality and that of others, since it helps me to gain Self Knowledge, Self Confidence, Self Esteem and a strong Radiance...
- I will avoid thinking in terms of 'good and evil,' 'positive and negative,' but will instead see everyone and everything just 'as is.' That's the highest form of respect...

- I will master my emotions; they will not master me...
- I will master any fear; fear will not master me...
- I will only worry about things I can change. I waste no mental energy on things I cannot change...

Action Plans

- My mentor(s) is (are) _____
- I will build and maintain MY Vision in Life. On paper!
- *Having* my Vision Statement is not that important: writing and re-writing it *is*. So I will make time for that, at least _____
- I will re-read my Vision Statement, at least _____
- I will constantly be on a 'mental diet,' deciding carefully about my intake of impressions from the outside world.
- Mental input I want to *increase* is _____
- Mental input I want to *decrease* is _____
- Mental input I want to *abandon* is _____
- Mental input I want to *maintain* is _____
- I will take silent time for reflection and planning in the following rhythm _____
- Yoga and Tai Chi Chu'an (or similar disciplines) enable a strong soul-mind-body connection and build flexibility, strength, focus and balance. I will practice both, at least _____

3. MY BODY PLAN

Vision

- My Body is the Temple of my Soul, my Ship of Life. I will nurture it and maintain it carefully, every day...
- I realize that my body will warn me when things go wrong, softly at first, louder later on. I will be alert to it signals...
- Whenever ill, I will be actively involved in the healing process. My vision on health and healing is _____

Action Plans

- My diet of foods and drinks is _____
- My food supplements are _____
- My exercise program is _____
- I will get sufficient fresh air by _____
- My rhythm of work, relaxing and rest is _____
- I will keep track (feedback) of the state of my body by _____

4. MY RELATION PLAN

Vision

- I will develop and maintain a strong Radiance...
- I will not do anything that might diminish my Radiance...
- I will not do anything that might diminish my Radiance...

- My Inner Smile will be my compass. It will never be stolen...

- I realize the danger of poisoning relationships and will eliminate them from my life, preferably by transforming them into blessing relationships...

- I will carefully manage expectations, both the ones I have about others and those that others might have about me...

- I will train myself in politely saying 'No,' instead of saying 'Yes' but then not make it true...

- I will be reliable for others, to the very best of my ability...

- I will not attribute negative labels to anyone... at least not longer than 90 seconds... (^-^)

Action Plans

- The most important people in my life are: _____
- Relations I would love to maintain: _____

- Relations I want to positively change are: _____
- Relations I want to end are: _____
- My other relations (neutral ones) are: _____
- I will maintain the contact data of all of my blessing relations carefully.
- I will make time every day to contact at least one of them; especially the one that 'pops up' in my mind spontaneously...
- I will keep friendships alive.
- The tool I will use to keep track of my obligations and promises is _____
- I will under-promise and over-deliver.
- If I can't keep a promise, I will inform 'the other one' in good time before my promised action falls due.
- Whenever I make a mistake, I will own up to it frankly, repair the damage and learn from it.
- I will not advise, nor help: I will only trigger personal growth...

5. MY HOME PLAN

Vision
- My home is my castle...
- My home is my extended body...
- My garden is my extended home...
- Both should be at the healthiest possible place...

- My home will have places for action, for gathering and for being silent...
- I will not be a prisoner of my home; I own (rent) the home, the home doesn't own me.
- 'Home is where your heart is'. If I have to leave my home for whatever reason, I will find a new one with the same qualities as written above.

Action Plans

- My home should be free of debt a.s.a.p.
- My home will be crispy fresh and clean.
- The maintenance plan of my home and garden: _____
- The financial plan for my home: _____

6. MY WEALTH PLAN

Vision

- I will keep the circle of abundance alive by giving the best I have to those who are worth it…
- I will not go for money alone: money is not a goal, but a means…
- I will not do just anything for money: I will do what I want to do…

- I will not hesitate to ask a reasonable price for what I do, not only in money…
- I will not waste my time on people and organizations that are not willing to give back…
- What I receive in return for what I do is an indication of my effectiveness; I will change plans if the indications are negative…
- I realize that earlier decisions are the source of my duties. I will change my decisions or keep my duties, not as a must, but as a part of the life I want to live…

Action Plans

- I will not 'just work': I will *give* with pleasure and pride.
- I will sow what I want to harvest.
- I aim to generate a net worth of $ _____ by _____
- My detailed plans for reaching that goal are _____
- I will reserve 10% of my income as a (pension) reserve.

- I will give away 10% of my income or time, preferably to goals connected to my own mission in life.

7. MY EARTH PLAN

Vision

- I am part of the environment. The environment is part of me...
- I am part of the society. The society is part of me...
- Planet Earth is my country...
- I will honor live, my relations, the environment, society and Planet Earth in all I do and to the best of my knowledge...

Action Plans

- Special contributions I want to make at home: _____
- Special contributions I want to make at work: _____
- Special contributions I want to make in my society : _____
- Special contributions I want to make in the world: _____

'Life isn't about finding yourself.

Life is about creating yourself.'

George Bernard Shaw

LIVING MY LIFE

I changed quite some aspects of my life, even while I was still 'Defining MY Vision.' I never realized before how interwoven Vision and Action are. From the very second you get a new insight, it doesn't matter about what, it starts influencing your actions. Your changed actions influence everything and everyone around you. Which influences you in its turn. Every step counts, and influences everything straight away. Amazing!

From the very first week after my meeting with Mentor in Ruckle Park, it seemed that almost everyone saw it. Many of my friends and relations asked 'What happened to you?' or 'Where have you been?'; and each time when I asked what they meant, the reply was that I looked 'way better.' That was encouraging!

Living your own life is simply executing the plans in your Vision Statement. It sounds simple, but it is really and art. Like every art it needs a lot of practice to master it. But it's so worthwhile: once you start, you experience for yourself what a huge difference your Vision Statement makes. It helps you at least in three crucial ways:

- *While writing*: words are formed in your mind... you write them down... and re-read them, maybe several times... you make some changes, and re-read the renewed sentences again... that goes on until you are satisfied. Meanwhile your brain is already making neuro-circuits for it.

- *When reading*: it is strongly recommended to read your Vision Statement several times a week, preferably aloud... and alone. Even when you know it's content by heart, still read it. Your brain is getting used to both the words and their meaning; the relevant brain circuits become stronger and stronger, just as if you were training for any sport. As a result your subconscious starts to help you to make the intentions you wrote down into a reality. In psychology this process is called 'autosuggestion.' And beyond any doubt: it works!

- *While living*: In tough times it helps you to stay focused, just by reading the words you wrote in better times.

Summarizing: Keep working on your Vision Statement and read it aloud as often as possible. Then observe what happens, and what will keep on happening. You might be pleasantly surprised.

Once your Vision Statement is more or less completed, living your life is nothing more and nothing less than 'just do it... live *your* vision!'

I found two aspects of 'Living My Life' really crucial: Rhythm and Feedback. I will share my vision about both.

RHYTHM

There are two types of time;
the unimportant one can be measured...

The time of clocks is so different from the time we experience. Waiting for your dentist, for example, can take forever, just like so many other stressful events in life. Other things can bring you 'in the gap' or 'in your element' and you might forget time completely, until you are shocked by looking at your watch...

Just because of these different aspects of time, it is important to create some rhythm. I created different rhythms in my life: the 'Planning Rhythm' and the 'Do Rhythm' as I have called them.

My '*Planning Rhythm*' is:

- Most of the December's last week is used for a *year planning*.
- Twice a year, spring and autumn, I will take 2 days to be alone and think about the *next half year*.
- Half of the third Friday or Saturday of each month is used for planning *the next month*.
- The *next week* is planned on Friday evening or Saturday morning.
- I finish every workday allowing about 10 minutes to plan *the next day* and to decide on what I call the Focus Task: the most important thing I have to *accomplish* (not just 'to do') on the next day.

A lot of planning, you might say. I don't think so. Once you get used to it, the actual planning doesn't take that much time. Moreover, it pays off and helps you to keep focused on what is really important to you.

For time-critical tasks '*Backward Planning*' works well: decide what you want to accomplish, and at what moment in time. Then make a list of all the steps that have to be taken, and when. Start by planning the last task leading up to completion: when does it have to start, in order to finish on time? Do the same for the penultimate task and so on. Revise the outcome back and forth until you have got '*a plan that says yes to you,*' a plan you can believe in.

One warning: since part of my own personality is a strong preference for improvisation, I have quite some problems to keep to any planning rhythm. But by thinking in Rhythms instead of a 'must' it becomes easier to stay on track. Moreover, having a proper planning allows you to improvise with peace of mind, since you can go back to your planning any time.

My '*Do Rhythm*' is actually a day and week rhythm: I divide each day into six parts: three main blocks - the morning, afternoon and evening - plus three sub-blocks about one hour before each main block, to start the day and to have two decent breaks. I focus on the main blocks and try to focus on one task, or set of tasks, in each of them. A week has $3 \times 7 = 21$ main time blocks; I start planning my week by manually drawing a table of 3 columns and 7 rows on a single piece of paper. I try to build in as much consistency as I can over the weeks. Nothing spectacular, but it works for me. Maybe for you as well.

2. FEEDBACK

If you have no specific goal,
you never can have a favorable wind.
Willem of Orange.

Feedback is essential. Especially to live your own life! Part of the Planning Rhythm is to see what went well and what can be improved in the future. Don't pose the question 'What went wrong?' but rather

'What can be improved?' especially when others are involved in your feedback. Very useful is to keep some simple graphics about how you are doing. If your weight for example is one of your points of feedback, you could just weigh yourself, but drawing the results on a graph by hand is *more* effective since you involve your Right Brain in the process instead of only the logical Left Brain.

I made a simple manual system for feedback for all of my seven plans. It works! Rhythm, Planning and Feedback keep me on track!

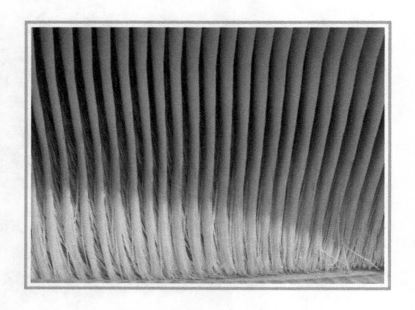

'Learn from yesterday, live for today,
hope for tomorrow.
The important thing is not to stop questioning.'

Albert Einstein

WHAT HAPPENED NEXT...

At the moment I write this last chapter, two years have passed since I met Mentor. What if I had not made that walk to Stanley Park that day? Or two hours later? Better not to think about it...

On the wall next to my desks hangs a framed document with the summary of Mentor's seven lessons:

See the miracle... and live it

'Know Thyself' and find your mentor

Be radiant... always... everywhere

Create abundance

Stay aligned... completely

Envision YOUR life... on paper

Live YOUR life... NOW!

At the other side hangs a framed quotation of Mentor's words:

'From the very moment you accept life's message

and make a definite decision to become who you really are,

—whatever it will take—

from that moment on, your life becomes an adventure again

and will reward you with new energy and inspiration,

some of it even instantly!'

Together they changed my life completely. Actually I changed my life myself, triggered by some lines in the notebook Mentor gave met and the two meetings with him. I am in good shape again, physically and mentally. I lost some 30 pounds in weight. I meditate, do Yoga and Tai Chi. I do regular cardio training and I love hiking at the weekends. Art and music have become an integral part of my life again.

My marriage has been saved: my wife was very surprised when we met again after the quite long time we had, by choice, not seen each other. '*Hey... You look great? How did you manage that?*,' was almost the first thing she said that day. And I told her. She was instantly intrigued and went on to go through more or less the same process that I had done. Comparing our mutual Personal Scans made clear to us a lot of things from our history; things that we had not understood at all when they happened. We found a good Certified Personality Coach who gave us even more insights, among others from the Relation Scan we had made.

I am a Certified Personality Coach now myself. And I love it! I quit my job and have never before earned such a nice income. A substantial part of that comes from the artwork I sell with increasing success.

I even wrote my first book...

Thank you for reading it!

May life's miracles bless you as much as they did and still do me...

'The difference between what we do

and what we are capable of doing,

would suffice to solve most of the world's problems.'

Mahatma Gandhi

Acknowledgements

The only fair way to express my deep gratitude to the many many people who helped me directly or indirectly in the writing of this book, would be by not mentioning names at all, because it's impossible to mention all of them. But I really need to mention a few people by name and some groups of people.

First and above all there is Anke, my Soulmate for so many many years. All insights in this book have arisen from our interaction. We've lived our life together as an adventure, avoided boring roads, dared to jump into a new life once in a while and stimulated each other in so many interesting ways, and with so many subjects. And that's what we still do, and hopefully will do to our last day. Anke's impact in this book is so manifest to me, that I asked her permission to give both of our names as the authors; she simply refused, since in her opinion only the actual writer should be mentioned. Let me put it this way: the 'vision' in this book has the two of us as authors, the 'action' - the physical writing - only one…

A huge part of our personal growth has stemmed directly from being parents. We are blessed with two great sons who not only bring light into our life but have taught us a lot, and continue to do so…

A special 'thank you' goes to our parents, brothers and sisters, other family members and our friends in the Netherlands, Canada and in several other countries in the world. They are part of our brains and our hearts.

Special gratitude goes also to all those who misused my trust, or cheated me or disappointed me in other ways, sometimes even with the best intentions: they allowed me to find out, and practice, how to deal with 'negative emotions'. Your lessons were hard, and at times very, very painful; but you helped me learn how to master my thoughts, feelings and emotions. If you are one of them - you know! - I am glad to say that there is no bitterness in my heart any longer.

Back in the 'nineties I wrote 4 books in my native language, Dutch. This is the first one in English. It was Will Menary, my editor in

Australia, who did more than just basic editing: he gave excellent feedback and helped make the book the 'great read' it is, as I've been told by readers in the meantime. Anders Schepelern from Wordy.com took care of the complex task of bridging three countries - and several different computers and programs - during the editing process. Well done, both!

I want to thank Pratap Chowdary and Deborah of BookGenie, India for their excellent service in typesetting this book and the creation of the ebooks.

Then my huge gratitude goes to all of my 'masters'. Many of them I've never met in person, but have learned from, solely through their words of wisdom in books, books written over a time span of about 3000 years... I name here just one who had a huge impact on this book: Carl Gustav Jung. His timeless insight let me understand many of the things that happened in my life. I often wonder how life would have been if I had learned his lessons 30 years earlier... That thought was one of the triggers to start writing this book. Jung is difficult to read; but I hope I've made him accessible for many people.

I hope, too, that this book will inspire both present and future generations to develop their own vision and live their own life!

About the author

Robert Bosman has a Doctorate in Business Economics, and is a Certified Public Accountant. He is a graduate of the Erasmus University of Rotterdam in the Netherlands.

He was formerly a partner and board member at Deloitte (the Netherlands), and a board member and executive consultant of several international organizations. His name is on two internet technology patents.

From 1990 onwards he became increasingly interested in psychology and philosophy, fields in which he is largely self-taught - an 'autodidact'. He has frequently been an invited speaker and guest lecturer at universities. He has written four books in the Dutch language about the 'quality of life and leadership', and developed a series of programs, services and courses in these fields.

In 2006 Robert and his wife Anke moved from the Netherlands to Canada. '*4000 Weeks*' is his first book in English. Robert is also the creator of *The Personal Scan, The Team Scan, The Job Scan, The Relation Scan, The Family Scan*, the related courses and the 32 *Personality Icons*.

Books from this author in Dutch:

- *The Synergy Scan* (1993 - De Synergie Scan)
- *The Time of your Life* (1995 - 't is Tijd om te Leven)
- *Strong Enough!* (1997 - Sterk Genoeg!)
- *Understanding People* (2005 - Mensenkennis)

Books from this author in English:

- *4000 Weeks* (2011)

Sources and credits

Related websites:

www.4000weeks.net

www.ThePersonalScan.net

www.2BeWise.net

Recommended books:

actual book list:

www.ThePersonalScan.com/resources/books

Picture credits and copyrights:

- Book cover front:
  Jeanine Groenewald - iStockPhoto.com
- page 4, 16, 82, 130:
  Osman Phillips Photography - cedarlanestudio.com
- page 10, 54, 114, 134:
  Natural Icons - visualphotos.com
- page 22:
  Stephen Walls - iStockPhoto.com
- page 124:
  Nautilus Shell Studios - iStockPhoto.com
- Page 69, brain halves in diagram:
  Robert Kudera, - iStockPhoto.com

All other pictures and diagrams: Robert Bosman

Music credits and rights:

page 55, 56: The Cats, Volendam / EMI Music

Printed in the USA
CPSIA information can be obtained
at www.ICGtesting.com
LVHW041140080924
790471LV00022B/155